The Radio Handbook

WITHDRAWN

The Radio Handbook is a comprehensive guide to radio broadcasting in Britain. Completely rewritten and updated for the second edition, using new examples, case studies and illustrations, it examines the various components that make radio, from music selection to news presentation, and from phone-ins to sports programmes. Carole Fleming explores the extraordinary growth of commercial radio, analyses the birth of digital audio broadcasting and Internet radio and evaluates their effects on the industry.

The Radio Handbook shows how communication theory informs everyday broadcasts and encourages a critical approach to radio listening and to radio practice. Addressing issues of regulation, accountability and representation, it offers advice on working in radio and outlines the skills needed for a career in the industry.

The Radio Handbook includes:

- interviews with people working at all levels in the industry, including programme controllers, news presenters and DJs
- examples of programming, including nationwide and local BBC, commercial radio, community and student stations
- chapters on radio style, the role of news, getting started in radio and the tools of broadcasting
- a glossary of key terms and technical concepts.

Carole Fleming is a senior lecturer in journalism at the Centre for Broadcasting and Journalism at the Nottingham Trent University. She has worked as a reporter and a producer for both BBC and ILR radio stations in the Midlands and the North East of England.

Media Practice

Edited by James Curran, Goldsmiths College, University of London

The *Media Practice* handbooks are comprehensive resource books for students of media and journalism, and for anyone planning a career as a media professional. Each handbook combines a clear introduction to understanding how the media work with practical information about the structure, processes and skills involved in working in today's media industries, providing not only a guide on 'how to do it' but also a critical reflection on contemporary media practice.

Also in this series:

The Radio Handbook

Second edition

Carole Fleming

London and New York

143943

1st edition published 1984
Reprinted 1996, 1999
2nd edition published 2002
by Routledge
11 New Fetter Lane, London EC4P 4EE

Simultaneously published in the USA and Canada
by Routledge
29 West 35th Street, New York, NY 10001

Routledge is an imprint of the Taylor & Francis Group

© 2002 Carole Fleming

Typeset in Times by
Florence Production Ltd, Stoodleigh, Devon
Printed and bound in Great Britain by
Biddles Ltd, Guildford and King's Lynn

British Library Cataloguing in Publication Data
A catalogue record for this book is available from the British Library

Library of Congress Cataloging in Publication Data
Fleming, Carole, 1955–
The radio handbook / Carole Fleming.–2nd ed.
    p. cm. – (Media practice)
Earlier ed. by Pete Wilby, 1994.
Includes bibliographical references and index.
1. Radio broadcasting–Handbooks, manuals, etc.   I. Wilby, Pete.
Radio handbook. II.   Title. III. Series.

PN1991.55.F54 2002
384.54--dc21

                                                        2001048944

ISBN 0–415–22615–5 (hbk)
ISBN 0–415–15828–1 (pbk)

For my parents
Tom and Margaret Fleming,
and to the memory of Robert Bradley,
Broadcast Journalism Student at the Nottingham Trent
University, who died on 16 December 2000.

Contents

....

Acknowledgements

....

One of the joys of writing this book was that I met so many people who share my passion for the medium and whose contributions have enriched this book and will hopefully inspire others to a better appreciation of radio. I have always felt that one of the distinguishing features of those who work in radio is that they are enthusiastic about the medium and keen to share their love of it with others, and researching this book has proved just that. I would like to thank everyone who has helped me to produce this edition of *The Radio Handbook* and in particular the following people: Chris Hughes and Phil Dixon from GWR; Colin Dudgeon for permission to use extracts from the GWR Brand Document; Sheldon James from Oak FM; Don Kotak from Sabras Sound; Jane Hill from Lincs FM; Sylvia Whalton from the Nottingham Trent University Students' Union; Katrina Gill from FLY FM; Fazil Malik from Radio Ramzan; Kate Squire, Alan Clifford, Emma Clifford and Pam Melbourne from BBC Radio Nottingham; Jane Franchi from BBC Scotland; Joanna Russell, Andy Twigge and Dick Stone at Trent FM; Andy Parfitt from Radio 1; Dan Thorpe from Metro Radio; Karen Morgan from Century 106FM; Vijay Sharma from the BBC Asian Network.

In addition I would like to thank my colleagues at the Centre for Broadcasting and Journalism for their support, particularly Gill Moore for advice on election coverage and legal matters, and the engineering team of Richard McShane, Mark Woodhead and Stephen Coates for technical advice.

Finally I would like to give heartfelt thanks to my sons, Dominic, Michael, Thomas and Sean Braithwaite, and my sister, Debbie Fleming, for all their encouragement and support throughout the writing of the book.

Introduction

....

Radio is a constantly evolving medium. Throughout the last century it has adapted to cultural and technological change to remain a popular and distinctive medium despite the growth of television, cinema, cable and satellite services, the ubiquity of recorded music, and even the Internet. So what makes radio so distinctive? The most obvious answer is its availability. Nine out of ten people in the UK listen to radio every week for an average of three hours a day, representing over one billion listening hours a week.[1] It is available in homes, shops, workplaces, cafés and cars and even to individuals walking in the countryside plugged into their personal steroes.

The downside to the widespread availability of radio is that it tends to be taken for granted. Because it is a medium that can be used while doing other things – whether driving the car or reading a book – it is widely regarded as a secondary medium which implies it is somehow less important than other media or lacking in some way. But this ignores radio's distinctiveness as a mass medium that addresses the individual. Radio creates a unique intimacy with its listeners who can interact with it through their imagination. As Andrea Hargrave's research into our listening habits shows (2000), radio is used as a friend to provide company, buck us up when we are feeling down or relax us when we are tired and tense. But it is a very undemanding friend that is always there and requires as much or as little of our attention as we are prepared to give.

For all that, however, radio is a business – something that is often overlooked because it is free to its listeners. Since the mid-1990s the radio industry in Britain has boomed. As well as national and local BBC services there are now almost 70 separate owners of independent radio licences[2] and although not yet widely listened to, digital radio is established and growing, as is radio via the Internet. The plethora of stations now available means competition within the industry to get and keep listeners is fierce. While this can be seen as beneficial in that it forces stations to have high standards of broadcasting, it can also be regarded as limiting the diversity of radio with stations adopting formats that appeal to the widest audience and sticking to tried-and-tested programming for fear of someone switching off.

The apparent contradiction of radio as a friend and also as a powerful business operation is just one of many contradictions that make radio a fascinating medium to study. The purpose of this book is to examine the organisational structures and operating principles that produce radio to reveal the complexities behind what is widely regarded as a simple medium. Its simplicity is apparent in the fact that all it requires is a microphone, a transmitter and a voice. But through interviews with those who work in the industry and an examination of communication theories that guide its production, the complexities of the medium become revealed and hopefully explained.

Radio is no longer confined to being received by a radio set: it is now available on many different platforms. For that reason Chapter 1 examines what can be termed 'mainstream' radio by looking at the way the BBC and commercial radio have developed in Britain, and in particular in examining the much-disputed terms of public service broadcasting and commercial broadcasting. It then goes on to examine the way radio is used and how this, along with audience research carried out by radio stations, influence programming. The chapter ends by profiling two small radio stations that illustrate how radio stations strive to connect with their audience by trying to offer a unique service.

The second chapter moves on to look at other forms of radio, from the latest digital services to small-scale community stations. This chapter illustrates the diversity of services available in Britain today and the potential radio has for entertaining, informing and educating – in short in making a difference to the lives of the people it reaches. The profiles of a student radio station and a community station show that while the airwaves are dominated by slickly produced pop-music stations, there is still a demand for radio that meets the needs of small very local groups.

This brings us to the identity of a radio station and how it is achieved – no matter whether a station is national or local, large or small, each has its own identity or brand designed to cater to a particular audience.

Chapter 3 looks in detail at how stations achieve their brand and examines the pros and cons of this practice. Does the brand of a radio station restrict its potential by making the programmes, presenters and jingles all sound the same? Or does it mean that a consistent standard is set that allows listeners to trust what they hear?

Of course an important part of any station's brand is the 'voice' it projects, and that is most obvious through its presenters. In Chapter 4 the role of the presenter is discussed by examining different presentation styles and analysing their effectiveness in promoting the station brand. The chapter ends by profiling different radio presenters and their programmes to illustrate how different styles target different audiences.

Another important part of the voice of a radio station – particularly a local radio station – is its news, and Chapter 5 examines the role of news on radio and how newsrooms operate. While the presentation and duration of news bulletins vary from station to station according to its target audience, essentially the news is compiled in the same way. For this reason this chapter describes the various elements that make up a news bulletin and what criteria are applied in the selection of news. It ends with a brief analysis of two news bulletins to demonstrate how the same news is shaped to cater for different audiences.

Probably the biggest change in radio over the past few years has been in the equipment it uses. Audiotape – once the life-blood of a station – has now disappeared from many stations and tasks ranging from editing audio to playing out programmes are now done by computer. In looking at the tools used in radio, Chapter 6 explains the new digital systems used and discusses their effect on radio output, as well as looking at the traditional tools of a microphone and recorder and explaining how to use them to get the best possible recording.

But while it is undeniable that technological changes do have an impact on programming, the fundamental strengths of radio – to interact with the audience, provide access to distant events, and provide up-to-date information on changing situations – remain the same. In Chapter 7 the way radio incorporates those strengths is discussed through an examination of types of programmes. This includes an examination of phone-ins, how they work and why they are so common; a look at sports programmes and the challenges they set broadcasters; election broadcasting; and how radio reacts to the unexpected.

Having examined the internal operations of radio, Chapter 8 then moves on to look at how radio represents its audience by examining three groups traditionally marginalised by the media: the old and young, ethnic minorities and women. It ends with an examination of the BBC World Service, which for many people represents the ideology not only of the BBC but also of the United Kingdom itself.

To a large extent the World Service, like other radio services in the UK, is formed by the laws and regulations that govern radio broadcasting. In Chapter 9 key laws that impact on broadcasting are outlined, followed by a discussion on the regulation of radio in Britain and the importance of self-regulation by broadcasters. The prospect of Britain gaining a new third tier of radio through 'access radio', as suggested in the Communications White Paper of December 2000, is also discussed.

The final chapter examines education and training for working in radio. Since the early 1990s, when many in-house training schemes were sacrificed for economic reasons, there has been a rise in courses provided by colleges, universities and commercial concerns. This chapter outlines various routes available to those who want to work in the industry.

While this book is by no means an exhaustive account of how radio operates in the UK, it is hopefully an insight into the key issues faced by broadcasters. There are already many books that analyse the theory of broadcasting. There are also books available about the practice of radio. What this book attempts is to show how what we actually hear when we switch on the radio is influenced by theory – from the structure of the 'radio day' to the selection of news. As with many other areas of the media, there is a certain amount of hostility between those who work in radio and those who theorise about it: practitioners tend to regard grand theories as irrelevant and theorists are often unaware of the pressures under which broadcasters have to work. This book attempts to bring both sides closer together by using the experiences of those working in radio to illustrate how theory informs their decisions and choices. In other words it is hoped that it will go some way towards explaining *how* radio is produced and *why* it is produced in that way.

Notes

1   Radio Authority, *Radio Regulation for the 21st Century*, June 2000: 7.
2   Ibid.: 2.

1 The renaissance of radio

....

I n the age of an abundance of media it might come as a surprise to some
that the oldest means of mass broadcasting – radio – is not only holding
its own but managing to increase its audience.[1] Radio is everywhere.
Apart from the BBC's five national stations and 39 local and regional
stations, Britain now has three national commercial radio stations,[2] and
almost 250 local and regional commercial stations. But that is only part
of the picture. Digital broadcasting began in 1998 bringing the potential
of hundreds of new stations bundled together in multiplexes and in June
2000 the first British-based Internet station – Storm Radio – was launched.

At the other end of the scale, technological advances and lower operating costs mean radio broadcasting is more accessible to more people.
Since the 1980s community radio stations have developed often operating
on a Restricted Service Licence (RSL) but nonetheless reaching a dedicated audience. Moreover, the Communications White Paper published in
December 2000 put forward plans for 'access radio' that will provide a
new third tier of radio run on a not-for-profit basis that should give community radio stations a new lease of life.[3] There are 70 student radio stations
usually run by enthusiastic student volunteers to provide a service for and
by students. Hospitals have their own stations and many supermarkets and
stores also run their own service. Radio is available as a digital service,
on the traditional analogue service, by cable, by satellite and over the
Internet.

More radio – less choice?

But more radio stations do not necessarily bring about more choice for listeners and sometimes the only way to distinguish between one station and another is the station ident (the jingle that identifies the station with its name and frequency). The majority of stations in Britain follow a very similar format dominated by music. As Andrew Crisell points out, 'Many students never listen to anything other than music radio and have only an inkling that stations still exist which broadcast a variety of "programmes" analogous to those they can watch on television' (1994: xi).

The reasons people listen to radio will be examined later in this chapter, and the following chapter will examine different kinds of radio. However, given that most people still listen to 'mainstream' radio, that is professionally produced radio for a mass audience broadcast on AM or FM, it is important to begin by examining those stations.

Broadly speaking, British radio falls into two categories: the BBC's 'public service' broadcasting and Independent Radio's commercial broadcasting. This division is not a clear-cut one, however, and the term 'public service broadcasting' is particularly problematic.

Although the BBC is publicly funded, it still needs to attract audiences to justify the licence fee and its very existence. Officially it is not in competition with commercial radio but many radio insiders believe the changes made to Radio 2 in 1998 with younger big-name presenters and more modern music were a direct assault on commercial radio's market. Moreover, the changes worked and in 2000 Radio 2 was the most listened-to station in the country.

But just because a station operates to make a profit does not preclude it from providing a service to the public. Indeed an audit in 2000 of the amount of time commercial radio devotes to public service announcements by the Commercial Radio Companies Association (CRCA) found that on average commercial stations spend two hours a week giving information about events in their area, with a further one and a quarter hours spent on social issues and charities. The CRCA say when this time is compared to paid-for advertising it works out at £104 million a year. 'Every week every commercial radio station supports its listeners in some way by educating, informing, fund raising or appealing on behalf of groups and individuals in need,' says Nick Irvine of the CRCA.[4]

For these reasons it is worth a closer examination of the two types of broadcasting to try to establish distinctions between them and see which 'public' is served by them.

Public service broadcasting[5]

For the first 50 years of its existence radio broadcasting in Britain was synonymous with the BBC. Originally a commercial company, the British Broadcasting Corporation was created in January 1927 by Royal Charter as a publicly funded organisation with sole responsibility for the provision of broadcasting in the United Kingdom. Its position as a monopoly with assured finance gave its first director general, John Reith, the time and resources to develop it free from commercial pressures, and its charter provided it with full editorial independence (Crisell 1994: 21).

However, being publicly funded also brought a responsibility for the BBC to 'serve' the public through programmes that 'inform, educate and entertain' and that are cost effective; and through targets that are continually reviewed by the government, who not only set the level of the licence fee but also determine the proportion of the fee given to the BBC and have the power to discontinue it altogether.

As Denis McQuail (1994) points out, there is no absolute definition of public service broadcasting; however, the Peacock Commission into broadcasting in 1986 came up with eight principles of the 'public service idea':

> Geographical universality of provision and reception; the aim of providing for all tastes and interests; catering for minorities; having a concern for national identity and community; keeping broadcasting independent from government and vested interests; having some element of direct funding from the public (thus not only from advertisers); encouraging competition in programmes and not just for audiences; and encouraging the freedom of broadcasters.
>
> (McQuail 1994: 126)

These principles are evident, to a greater or lesser extent in each case, in the way the BBC currently operates as their statements in *The BBC Beyond 2000* make clear.[6]

> Public funding through the licence fee establishes an implicit contract with every household in the nation that the BBC will set standards of quality and diversity . . . And because BBC services are not competing for commercial revenues they can afford to meet a far wider range of these expectations, pushing the boundaries of public service broadcasting further, testing success not just by ratings – though no service succeeds unless it attracts a substantial audience – but according to

whether it offers something of real value to the audience that is not guaranteed elsewhere.

It is in striving to balance programmes that are 'popular' with listeners and those which provide the sort of things 'not guaranteed elsewhere' that causes the most problems for the BBC. It tackles this through what Stephen Barnard calls complementarity. 'Complementarity in radio services means the provision of programming which dovetails, rather than directly competes, with that of other stations' (Barnard 2000: 32). In other words, the BBC designs each of its radio services with a distinct audience in mind so that every interest can be catered for within the BBC family, and while continuing to 'inform, educate and entertain' listeners and provide what is seen to be lacking in commercial radio.

This is most noticeable in the speech-based stations of Radio 4 and Radio 3 that provide radio drama and documentaries unavailable elsewhere. However, it can also be argued that Radio 1 also provides a service not available elsewhere since its revamp in the 1990s from a pop-music station to a 'youth' station targeting 15–25-year-olds with a mix of new music and social-issue campaigns on drugs, unemployment and student life. Andy Parfitt, the controller of Radio 1, believes part of the public service his station provides involves promoting new talent that can be ignored by the globalising tendencies of the music industry. 'I think public service broadcasting is absolutely crucial in stimulating regional and cultural diversity and providing a platform for new artists and new talent,' he says.[7] 'At the same time it can't be a niche activity. In order to be relevant it has to be a certain size and have a certain reach and be appreciated by a number of people, so you have to get a balance between great big global acts that are everyone's favourites and new acts that happen to come from South London or Manchester or Nottingham.' And he acknowledges that the public service aspect of the station is not just confined to the music. 'Predominantly we are a music station but because we reach out into people's lives all the time – we're the sound track to their lives – then what we also provide in terms of news and speech and the social action features enriches the output and gives it depth,' he says. 'It doesn't ever dominate but if it weren't there it would be sorely missed.'

In a similar way BBC local radio provides a service with a high level of speech and music programmes aimed at the over 45s who are a group until recently largely ignored by other broadcasters.

Commercial broadcasting

Commercial radio, as its name suggests, is run to make a profit by selling airtime to advertisers. It began in Britain in 1973 with a network of local stations overseen by the Independent Broadcasting Authority. In its early days the stations were similar to the BBC's music-based stations, except they carried advertising, partly because so many of the new stations' staff were former BBC employees but also because of the way it was regulated.

From the beginning the IBA imposed certain public service obligations on stations by insisting they carry a full news service and provide programming to appeal to all age groups and reflect the diversity of their community (Barnard 2000: 53). What this meant was that commercial radio could not deliver a specific audience to advertisers, so its appeal to them was limited. The prospect of making a profit was further hindered by what Andrew Crisell calls the 'unnecessarily high technical standards' (1994: 36) required by the IBA and high transmitter rents paid to it.

On top of this the birth of new stations occurred during a period of recurrent recession when advertising generally hit a slump, and at a time of increased competition from new forms of television – breakfast television, Channel 4, cable and satellite – as well as an increase in land-based pirate stations who were free from regulation and so could provide advertisers with targeted audiences (Crisell 1994: 37).

The 1990 Broadcasting Act changed all that. Ownership and investment regulations were considerably relaxed, as well as the public service requirement, and three national commercial stations were proposed along with a promise to expand local and regional services. The Act also saw the disbanding of the IBA and the setting up of the Radio Authority[8] whose main tasks were:

> To plan frequencies; to appoint licensees with a view to broadening listener choice and to enforce ownership rules; and to regulate programming and advertising.
>
> (Radio Authority Fact Sheet Number One)

In particular the promise to 'broaden listener choice' brought hope that commercial radio would at last be able to cater to a wide range of interest groups by being freed from its requirement to cater to everyone in its transmission area. The reality, however, is that most commercial radio stations target very similar audiences – the ones identified by advertisers as having the most spending power and therefore the ones they want to reach with their message. The size of radio audiences is important to advertisers but equally important is the audience profile that gives the demographic picture of the average listener. There would be little point in advertising disposable nappies, for example, on a station whose audience consisted mainly of 55-year-old men. For that reason commercial stations, especially since 1990, target a specific audience in order to 'sell' it to advertisers. In other words the audience of commercial radio is a commodity sold to advertisers to fund radio stations whose purpose is to attract and keep a specific demographic group of people.[9] To paraphrase Jean Seaton, 'commercial radio does not produce programmes it produces audiences' (Curran and Seaton 1991: 212).

Of course the BBC also targets specific audiences, but its targeting is on the basis of interest. Commercial radio needs advertising to exist so they target audiences based on the people advertisers want to reach and tailor their programmes accordingly. The effectiveness of audience targeting is shown by the fact that in 1990 radio had a 2 per cent share of all advertising revenue, but by 2000 its share had increased to 6 per cent (Mills 2000).

For radio groups like GWR, the target audience is 25–34-year-olds, as the managing director of Leicester Sound, Phil Dixon, explains:

> That sort of age group is very aspirational for the age group both above and below it. The younger ones want to be it and the older ones like to think they're still a bit trendy and young. It all comes together in that age bracket and that's the age we target. They've got money to spend and advertisers want them to spend it with them, so from a revenue/business perspective it's important because that's what advertisers want.[10]

Radio is big business and, while the number of stations continues to grow, there is increasing consolidation with groups buying out small independent stations which then adopt the group's format. This is leading to a homogenisation of the sound of radio with 'local' stations controlled from group headquarters rather than the place their audience is based.

The biggest group is GWR based in Bristol. In October 2000 it owned 36 local stations from Plymouth Sound to Ram FM in Derby, as well as the national station Classic FM. The advantages of being a large group are that resources can be pooled to cut down costs; sales teams can sell advertising for several stations at the same time; news can be delivered from a central newsroom; managers can oversee more than one station; programmes can be shared.

The disadvantage is that there is little to distinguish the output from Plymouth or Derby except the occasional local accent and the content of the news: the schedule, playlists and style of presentation are the same across the whole group. Moreover, as the format of large groups like GWR is seen to bring in revenue, other smaller stations are influenced by it and adopt it in the hope of increasing their listeners which they then 'sell' to advertisers. The result is that radio all begins to sound the same and as a medium its potential to inform and entertain other than through music is being ignored outside the BBC.

Supporters of commercial radio point out that the BBC can afford to take a more varied approach to broadcasting because it is not dependent on audience figures to produce advertising revenue in order to survive. They also point out that while the BBC national network is holding its own with a 51.1 per cent audience share compared to 47.2 per cent for national commercial radio, on a local and regional level the BBC only manages an 11.2 per cent share compared to the 38.8 per cent of local and regional commercial stations.[11] In other words, commercial radio appears to be giving audiences what they *want* to hear rather than what radio managers think they *ought* to hear.

Nonetheless the overall impact of commercial radio catering to advertisers creates a situation where there is less diversity of programmes and minority interests and groups are ignored. As Stephen Barnard points out,

> The classic critical argument against commercialisation of mass communications media is that pursuit of advertising revenues encourages programming assumed to appeal to the greatest number, thereby marginalising less popular tastes and interests. It creates an environment most conducive to reception of the advertising message, leading to programming that is undemanding, unchallenging and pacifying.
>
> (Barnard 2000: 51)

The bigger picture

Taken as a whole, radio broadcasting in Britain could be regarded as covering all tastes by offering commercial and public service models.

Moreover, the number of small stations catering for sparsely populated areas has increased dramatically since the 1990 Broadcasting Act. In Scotland, for example, 16 new commercial stations have gone on air since 1991, including bilingual stations like Isles FM on the Isle of Lewis, and Heartland FM in Perthshire.

Digital radio also appears to be offering more choice with most of the current multiplexes carrying a mixture of different types of music-based stations, and in large metropolitan areas an Asian service as well.

However, there are still many groups in Britain who are ignored by the currently available radio stations. Apart from a handful of Asian radio stations and the BBC's Asian Network, most ethnic minorities are not catered for by mainstream radio especially outside large metropolitan areas like London and Birmingham.[12] Regardless of ethnicity, children under 15 and adults over 65 are not catered for in any direct way, although, as Chapter 8 discusses in more detail, this is beginning to change. Even music-based stations are very narrow in the range of music they play. There is very little live music, and outside major cities even jazz and country music, which both have enormous followings, are barely acknowledged, let alone more 'specialist' forms of music.

As Denis McQuail points out, the mass media are of considerable importance to modern societies in part because they are

The source of an ordered and public meaning system which provides a benchmark for what is *normal*, empirically and evaluatively; deviations are signalled and comparisons made in terms of this public version of normality.

(McQuail 1994: 1)

From its beginning the strength of radio was that it opened up the world to people. It was no longer necessary to 'be' somewhere in order to experience an event – it was brought to you through your radio. The views and attitudes of different groups in society became available to those outside that group; the voices of politicians, trade unionists, archbishops, the homeless and the 'ordinary' person were all heard directly by thousands of people, whose 'experience' of society was enlarged. While this is not to suggest that this created greater understanding of different parts of society, it did provide greater knowledge of it. Similarly this is not to suggest a return to the paternalistic Reithian approach to radio as a means to 'improve' the masses. What is being suggested is that the majority of radio stations now broadcast to a similar but narrow part of society, and in so doing they are promoting a narrow definition of what constitutes 'normal', which could lead to increasing numbers of people being seen as marginal and becoming alienated. As Robert McLeish writes, 'radio should surprise' (1994: 6). Unfortunately, in these days of format radio it seldom does.

The listener

But despite the increasing sameness of radio it is still a popular medium with 90 per cent of the population tuning in for an average of 24 hours a week (Leonard 2000). As Shingler and Wieringa (1998) point out, radio is very much taken for granted these days but that does not detract from the qualities that make it so enduringly popular.

Chief among these qualities is radio's ability to talk directly to the audience. Although it is a mass medium it does not address the 'mass' but the individual. In this way radio is an intimate medium, one that listeners feel is addressing them, even when they know that thousands of people are listening at the same time. This was not always the case, however, as Paddy Scannell notes:

> The talk that prevailed in early broadcasting in the UK was monologue rather than dialogue, in which selected speakers spoke at length from the studio to absent listeners on predetermined scripted topics.
>
> (1991: 2)

These days, however, radio is widely used for companionship, and the majority of radio listening occurs when people are alone (Hargrave 2000: 13). As a companion, radio is particularly undemanding and most people use it as a background to other activities, particularly driving the car, and because of this it is often referred to as a 'secondary medium' which implies that it is somehow lacking and inferior. But part of its strength comes from its ability to be used while doing other things, and one of the reasons given for the increase in audiences is that computer users listen to it while working on their PCs or surfing the Internet (Leonard 2000).

More than any other medium radio allows you to experience it while doing other things, but that does not lessen its effectiveness. The power of radio to create moods goes back to its earliest days when the BBC created the Forces Programme in 1940 'to maintain the morale of troops forming the British Expeditionary Force in France' (Crisell 1986: 22), followed by programmes like 'Music While you Work' to help boost production in munitions factories. The fact that radio can be heard in shops, cafés, garages, offices and factories suggests it is still used in this way.

In research by the Broadcasting Standards Commission and the Radio Authority it was found that one of the main uses of radio was to alter the listener's mood. It is used to help people relax before going to bed; to energise them before going for a night out; to stimulate them and give them something to think about; and to lighten their mood if they feel a bit down (Hargrave 2000: 12).

Another strength of radio is that it is immediate. Listeners tune in regularly for traffic updates, and those with car radios that have a Radio Data System (RDS) have regular traffic flashes displayed automatically. Moreover, despite advances in technology that allow television to broadcast live from almost any location, because radio is easier to access – in cars, the workplace, through personal headsets – it is ideal for keeping people informed about breaking news stories.

It is also a very responsive medium. Requests and comments from listeners can be made by telephone, fax and email and included almost immediately in the programme, making listeners feel part of it. This is particularly true of phone-in discussions where the programme is regarded as a place for the audience to express their views.

> They were not considered to be a vehicle for the presenter's own views – this was not thought to be appropriate. It was felt the presenter's role should be neutral and their own view should be expressed only to aid the flow of the conversation and start or maintain a debate.
>
> (Hargrave 2000: 19)

Radio also responds to the audience by making changes to its schedules as a result of market research or because of falling audience numbers. The way this is done is worth closer examination, if only because the industry spends so much time and money on it.

Audience research

As previously mentioned, the size of radio audiences is important to commercial radio because they sell advertising on this basis, but it is also important to the BBC as a way to measure the popularity of their stations and thereby help to justify the continuation of the licence fee. For this reason the BBC and the Commercial Radio Companies Association (CRCA) set up a radio industry research company – RAJAR Ltd – in 1992 which they jointly own. Prior to this, audience data were collected by two separate services: the BBC Daily Survey which monitored BBC radio, and the Joint Industry Committee for Radio Audience Research (JICRAR) for commercial stations. The problem with this was that different methodologies and the fact the figures were not independently produced cast doubt on their accuracy. As RAJAR (Radio Joint Audience Research) points out:

> The creation of RAJAR has greatly improved overall confidence in radio as a medium over the years since 1992, principally because it provides a single accepted measure of radio listening.
>
> (www.rajar.co.uk)

Understandably, measuring radio audiences is complicated: radio can be listened to virtually anywhere and there are literally hundreds of station areas to survey. The cost to the radio industry for this service is almost £4 million a year.

RAJAR produce listening figures every three months based on the response from 3,000 selected respondents who each compile a seven-day diary of their listening habits. While this may seem a time-consuming and old-fashioned method of measuring audiences, because radio is listened to in a variety of locations it is still felt to be the most reliable. Several types of radio-meters are being developed, but because they require respondents to carry or wear the meter at all times, their effectiveness is still in doubt.

The problem with this kind of information, however, is that it only measures the number of people tuning in to a particular station. It is unable to tell whether the output was liked or even 'listened' to as opposed to just being on in the background. Because of this stations also have to do market research to show what kind of programmes are preferred at what times of the day and night.

For the BBC this research has two main purposes. The first is that it helps them to adapt their programmes to what listeners say they want in the hope it will increase their share of the audience. The second is that it fulfils their obligation to be seen to respond to the licence-paying public. For that reason as well as traditional market research carried out by its own Audience Research Department, the BBC operates a series of audience 'councils' who meet periodically to give their opinions directly to BBC managers. Kate Squire, the editor of BBC Radio Nottingham, says the local radio council is 'a great source of information and help'. The 12 member councils meet every two months and follow a nationally agreed business plan about what programmes will be discussed. The councils are made up of 'ordinary' listeners, who go through a formal application process and an interview before joining the council. 'What I usually do is give them a listening exercise before they come for the interview, so it might be to listen to the mid-morning show and comment on this that and the other,' Kate Squire explains. 'We don't want people who just say everything's great and we think you're wonderful. We want people to be constructively critical but we don't want people from pressure groups – we want normal radio listeners who don't have a particular axe to grind, with a nice geographical spread around the county and a good age range and a good ethnic mix.'

The meetings are usually between the council and the editor of the station and are bound by strict confidentiality. 'We often talk very openly about presenters and programmes,' Kate Squires explains. 'Sometimes my news editor will come but usually it's just me because the meeting needs to be very open and the rule is what's said doesn't go out of that room.'

As well as commenting on programmes, the council is also used to help with outside broadcasts and special events like charity phone-in weekends and the station's Christmas pantomime.

In Scotland, Ireland and Wales there are National Broadcasting Councils, and in England audiences are represented by the English National Forum as well as the regional and local advisory councils. There is also an ongoing project called 'The BBC Listens' which comprises public meetings, special programmes and audience research. The comments from all this research are then sent to the BBC Board of Directors.

Audience research by commercial radio is done in a less comprehensive manner. Because it is expensive, small stations tend to use it before the station is launched and then only when a problem is perceived through a consistent drop in the RAJAR figures. Groups like GWR, however, undertake continual audience research most of which focuses on musical preferences.

Every week GWR speaks by telephone to hundreds of people, aged from 20 to 34, about their musical tastes. Each respondent is asked to identify their current musical preferences from a shortlist of musical 'clusters', and then asked for their opinions on a list of current songs. The learning from this ongoing research helps in the construction of our group playlists.

(GWR brand document)

As well as this, however, research is done into the lifestyle of their audiences and their interests. This is used to help shape programmes, particularly the news (see Chapter 5), and to provide advertisers with information about the kind of people listening.

Ways of listening

However, there is evidence that the way we listen to radio is changing. In 1994 research into radio audience attitudes showed that people tend to find a station they like and stick with it, developing a loyalty to a station's style, presenters and schedules (Hargrave 1994). Six years later it was found that although some presenters elicited strong loyalty, with listeners changing to other stations to follow them, there was not so much loyalty to stations (Hargrave 2000). This is reflected in data from the Radio Advertising Bureau that shows the average number, radio stations listened to nationally each week rose from 1.9 in 1994 to 2.3 in 2000.

The most obvious reason for this is that there is now more choice, and curiosity makes listeners dip in and out of different stations. But another factor is that it is now easier to change stations because of technological advances that allow pre-programming, so that a station can be changed at the touch of a button rather than having to fiddle with a dial.

This means broadcasters have to work even harder not only to get an audience but also to keep its interest. While this is a constant challenge for established radio stations, new stations face the added problem of making people aware of their existence in the first place, as well as tempting them to stay tuned. For most stations this requires a period of trial and error, and as the following profile of Oak FM in Leicestershire shows, constant tweaking of schedules and formats. The second profile of the Asian station Sabras Sound shows how small stations can build a dedicated audience by being responsive to the local community.

Profile | 107 Oak FM, Loughborough
Radio for the locality

Oak FM is one of a growing number of small radio stations set up to cater for a small town/rural population who feel ignored by larger local radio stations. As its station director Sheldon James explains, 'I think radio's got an additional tier to it now. You've got national and regional and local stations but there's another tier underneath those stations made up of smaller stations like Oak FM that centre heavily on one particular area within the larger local station's transmission service area.'

The station went on air in February 1999 and broadcasts to a potential audience of around 120,000 over-15-year-olds. Competition from other commercial stations is strong because of the location of Loughborough between three major urban areas. Trent FM in Nottingham, Ram FM in Derby and Leicester Sound all owned by the GWR group, as well as the regional station Century 106FM owned by Capital Radio, can be heard in the area, but Sheldon James does not see this as a problem. 'At least our competition locally is all doing the same thing, so if we want to be different there's a stronger chance of us picking up people who don't like what they're doing,' he says.

The station was created by a consortium of local businesses, including the local newspaper which provided good advance publicity for the new station. The station also had a 'trial run' before officially launching, through a 14-day restricted service licence (RSL) that was used to gauge local interest. This was further backed up by market research in the area to try to find what people most wanted from a local station.

However, the station was not just created on the whims of the population. Twenty per cent of its shares are owned by the Echo Newspaper Series who belong to the Midland Independent Newspaper group, now owned by the Mirror Group. A further 20 per cent of the shares belong to Milestone Pictures, whose chairman is an experienced radio and television broadcaster, that also runs Show FM, a company that specialises in RSLs at agricultural shows and other special events. Another 10 per cent of the shares belong to Non Metropolitan Radio, a radio consultancy headed by experienced broadcasters. So, although the local population was consulted, the creation of the station was also guided by experienced broadcasters.

Having gained the licence, the next step was to find suitable premises for the station. In line with many new stations, Oak FM found premises on a small industrial estate on the edge of the town centre, turning the all-purpose shell into a reception area, a large open-plan office for the news team, sales team and station manager, and two fully operational studios.

Building and equipping the studios with the latest digital technology was the biggest expense, although Sheldon concedes that being a radio station is easier than it used to be. 'New technology makes life easier and cheaper once you've invested in the initial technology,' he says, but adds it is still a specialist job. 'It's a different way of doing things. If you're editing a cut on a digital editing machine it still takes time to find the right bits – there's no magic wand – it still takes skill and precision.'

Although the station uses the industry standard Selector software to programme music, it was decided to augment this with a traditional studio desk. 'We use a system called Bar Code which is fader operated so when you're at the desk it's like being a "proper" DJ,' says Sheldon. 'One of the reasons we went for a fader system is that a touch screen is located either to the left or right of the desk and every time you want to change something you have to turn your head which takes you away from the microphone. This system avoids that and gives you all the advantages of digital play-out.'

According to the licence application submitted to the Radio Authority, the station aimed to provide a minimum of 20 per cent speech in its daytime output. Sheldon James admits that in its first year of operating, before he joined the station, this was higher with features like the chief executive of the County Council doing guest slots every week, and lunch-time phone-in programmes. But this style of broadcasting appealed to older listeners too much. 'We were typically hitting a 55-year-old male,' Sheldon explains. 'I looked at the sound of the station and tried to reposition us a bit because we had too many older listeners and we needed to lower the age we appealed to. Our target now is a 35-year-old female and I would like to think that we would never broadcast anything that would make her switch off.' The current format reflects this change, and while there are still studio guests they tend to be visiting celebrities rather than local dignitaries.

However, despite these changes Oak FM tries to be involved with the local community as much as possible through charity drives, events like the switching on of the Christmas lights, and interacting with the audience through listeners' phone calls, faxes and emails. The presenters are key to this. 'A good presenter is someone who is the same on-air as they are off-air – people who don't go into "Smashy and Nicey" mode,' explains Sheldon. 'They have to be people who have a knowledge of the area and for us – being a small team – someone who is a team player, who is just as interested in passing on leads to the sales department as becoming a star on the radio.'

The news is also a key part of being part of the community, and the station employs three full-time journalists who do hourly bulletins between 7 a.m. and 6 p.m. every weekday, with headlines on the half hour during breakfast news, the lunch-time segment and drive-time. The hourly bulletins are four minutes long with extended bulletins at 1 p.m. and 6 p.m.

'News is particularly important because it is a very good way for us to be local,' comments Sheldon. 'Leicester Sound was the main local station but they don't have the resources to cover Loughborough in as much depth as we can, so it's important for us to have some very strong local angles in our news and news which is relevant to our target audience.'

At weekends, in common with the majority of local stations, local news runs from 6 a.m. to 2 p.m. with IRN bulletins at other times. Weekends see a change to schedules in other ways too with a Saturday afternoon programme that has match reports from sporting events, although these feature less now than in the early days of the station, in line with their target listener. 'It's a music-based show that keeps people informed about what's happening without sport dominating it,' says Sheldon. 'We try to provide a service that doesn't make people switch off.'

Keeping the station prominent has also prompted other changes, with a new logo reflecting a 'show business quality', a four-wheel-drive station jeep to do promotions, and plans for a web site. The station is also negotiating with the Radio Authority to change the position of its transmitter, currently on top of the tower of Loughborough University, to a site that will make its signal stronger in its core area.

Although small, the 16 people who work at Oak FM are all genuinely enthusiastic about the station and its potential, but that does not detract from what Sheldon James sees as the bottom line. 'It's important that we serve the community,' he says, 'but it's crucially important that we never forget that this is a business and we have to make money. The reality is that any business is there to make money – it might be radio and you might like to provide great entertainment for people and you might like to have good promotions – but the bottom line is it's there to make money.'

Profile   Sabras Sound
Radio for the community

The word 'sabras' means 'all tastes' in Hindi and it was with that in mind that Don Kotak used it to name his weekly two-hour show on the first commercial radio station in Leicester in 1980. The show is now a 24-hour commercial station in its own right with what the *Sunday Times* has dubbed 'the keenest radio fans in the country' tuning in for over 19 hours a week on average.[13]

The station broadcasts throughout Leicestershire mainly in English and Hindi (the main language of the Indian subcontinent), but also in Gujarati, Punjabi and Bengali. It provides a mix of Indian music, local and international news, features, Bollywood gossip and even religious programmes. The station's main shareholder and managing director is broadcaster and businessman Don Kotak, who says the station's popularity comes from knowing the local population so well. 'We have designed programmes to suit the mix of the local population,' he explains. 'If I were sitting in Bradford running an Asian station I would not programme it in the same way as I have done here.'

Asian broadcasting in Britain was pioneered in Britain on BBC Radio Leicester in 1976. By the time commercial radio came along the city's Asian population had programmes for five hours a week. Don Kotak agreed to move to the new station, providing its two-hour programme did not clash with the BBC's, so that overall the city would have more Asian programmes. 'It was always my ambition to have a 24-hour Asian radio station in Leicester,' he says.

By 1992 the dream looked possible, and the Radio Authority agreed that the Midland Radio Group who owned Leicester Sound could change their AM 'golden oldies' frequency into a 24-hour Asian radio station. At this stage, however, business took the dream over, and instead of Don Kotak being allowed to run the new station as had been expected, a deal was struck with the London Asian station Sunrise Radio to take it over, and Don and his team walked out. However, the Sunrise broadcasts were not popular, and after being approached by various groups in the Asian community, Don made a successful application for the AM licence for the city when it came up for renewal and began broadcasting in September 1995.

The station is based in a beautifully converted church in the middle of Leicester's 'Golden Mile' Asian district. The body of the church has been converted into a large open-plan area with settees and coffee tables looking into the station's three studios that still have the old archways and stained-glass windows of the original building. This area is used for any live broadcasts involving an audience, but it also allows shoppers a chance to pop into the station and see the presenters at work. 'They treat us like a community centre,' laughs Don.

But the reality is that the station's output has been carefully selected to cover all sections of the Asian community. 'I have to direct our programming to reflect a huge range of requirements that mainstream stations don't have to,' explains Don. 'We have to reflect young and old, address religious requirements, different cultural music requirements, and then we have to address the language balance between how much English we use and how each community's language will be used. We have gone out not to be antagonistic to anybody but to recognise the requirements of all sections of the Asian community.'

To that end ISDN lines have been installed in the city's mosques and temples so that they can broadcast directly from there. The Sabras 'day' begins at 4 a.m. with three hours of religious broadcasting from Sikhs, Muslims and Hindus who have an hour each that is rotated each week. This is followed by a three-hour breakfast show in English that is 'very zany and fast moving'. The bulk of the day is broadcast in Hindi and targets housewives, factories and the elderly, before returning to English broadcasting for drive-time. Evening and weekend broadcasts have programmes in Punjabi, Bengali and Gujarati.

The station takes IRN news on the hour but supplements it with in-house news from 7 a.m. to 6 p.m. which is a mix of local news and news from the Indian subcontinent, three of which are in Hindi to cater to elderly listeners.

For all the success of Sabras Sound, Don Kotak is frustrated at the lack of choice in radio for Asians. 'An English person has a choice of what radio station they want to listen to – the Asian listener doesn't have that choice. It's between Sabras and the BBC,' he explains. 'The BBC is still very speech-orientated and still behind in terms of slickness and trendy-sounding if you like, so we have a great responsibility to the listeners.'

And Don is also aware that the demographic profile of the population is changing. 'In my opinion Asian radio is at a huge crossroads – we are where mainstream radio was in the mid-80s,' he says. 'We've now got 20 years of broadcasting under our belt and we have to restructure our programmes to make sure the youngsters not only come to our stations but stay there. We're losing a lot of youngsters to mainstream radio because Asian youngsters don't relate to Asian music. This is a huge problem because we have to address the needs of the whole community but we have to be mindful that the population is changing.'

For Don the solution is to have more radio stations that could tailor their output to specific age groups. Ideally he would like an FM service for younger Asians, and continue the AM service for more traditionally minded people but he realises this will probably never happen. Of the five Asian radio stations in Britain, only the one in Bradford broadcasts on an FM frequency.

'We're stuck – we want to expand but there's nowhere to go,' says Don who is aware that the days of one radio station catering for 'all tastes' may soon be ending.

Notes
....

1   In the first three months of 2000 commercial radio in Britain increased its audience by one million, while the BBC added an extra 400,000 to its listeners. Quoted in 'Ad hoc: Advertisers Going Ga-Ga for Radio' by Dominic Mills, Tuesday, 23 May 2000 at www.electronictelegraph.co.uk.

2   Atlantic 252 also broadcasts to Britain but it is based in Ireland and does not come under the control of the Radio Authority or other controls that apply to British-based stations.

3   See Chapter 9 for a detailed discussion on the Communications White Paper and access radio.

4   CRCA press release, 14 September 2000.

5   For a fuller history of the BBC see Crisell (1997) and Scannel and Cardiff (1991).

6   Full document available at www.bbc.co.uk.

7   Author interview with Andy Parfitt, July 2001.

8   A fuller explanation of the role of the Radio Authority is given in Chapter 9.

9   See Dallas Smythe (1997) for a fuller explanation of the commodification of audiences.

10   Author interview with Phil Dixon, managing director of Leicester Sound, October 2000.

11   Figures for second quarter of 2000. Source: RAJAR.

12   There are minority stations available by satellite, for example Tamil Radio and Television, and cable, for example Radio Orient.

13   *Sunday Times*, Culture Section, 15 February 1998. Since 1998 the station's average listening has increased from 14.4 hours to 19.2 hours (RAJAR for second quarter 2000).

2 The radio revolution

....

Radio is endlessly adaptable. Despite challenges from other media, radio continues to be popular because of its ability to adapt to changes. Technological determinists might claim that the changes are due to advances in technology like stereo broadcasting, the transistor radio and the use of FM and digital frequencies for better-quality sound. But a closer examination of these technological developments shows that most were available long before they were applied. What brought about their application is what Brian Winston calls 'supervening social necessities' (1995: 68) which act as accelerators in the development of media and other technology.

The transistor, for example, was first discovered in 1948 but it did not become widely used until the 1960s when Britain was more affluent. The new transistors made radio portable at a time when society was becoming increasingly mobile and the younger generation was emerging as a distinct consumer group. Radio responded to this by tailoring programmes to match the lifestyle of the time. Similarly, the first FM transmitter was opened in Kent 1955 but it was not until the 1980s that stations began to switch to the better-quality frequency, mainly because the Independent Broadcasting Authority insisted that franchise holders provide separate services on AM and FM. The supervening social necessity in this case was the need to find more spectrum combined with that of producing better-quality sound to meet the expectations of audiences used to ever more sophisticated sound systems. As Stephen Barnard notes, 'radio's ability to survive in a competitive media environment has always depended on how well broadcasters tap into social, cultural and technological change' (2000: 17).

The adaptability of radio is clear not only in the many ways it is broadcast but also in the way it is used for so many different purposes. As this chapter shows, the different forms that radio has make it suitable to reach people in a myriad of ways from mass global audiences to those in closed communities.

Digital radio

Even before digital radio was broadcast it was hailed as the saviour of radio. Here at last was a system that delivers 'pure' sound free from atmospheric and electrical interference, and uses new frequencies that allow the creation of new stations at a time when space on the existing AM and FM frequencies is scarce.

Initially developed in Britain by BBC engineers in the 1970s, Digital Audio Broadcasting (DAB) uses new high-frequency bands, with several services carried in one block of frequencies called a 'multiplex'. Britain has seven multiplexes divided between the BBC and commercial operators, with each multiplex typically carrying ten services.

The sound quality of digital radio has been compared to the different sound quality between vinyl and CDs. It works by converting the radio signal into binary digits (0s and 1s) in a way that is resistant to interference using a Single Frequency Network that allows the same frequency block of spectrum to be reused throughout a large service area. This means there is more space for extra services, and because all the transmitters are using the same frequency to broadcast the same digital radio signal, there is no need to retune the radio when driving. Digital radio also allows extra information to be sent to the LCD display of radio sets. This can be anything from the name of the band that is playing to stock market prices or the telephone number of advertisers.

The BBC began its digital broadcasting in 1995 simulcasting its five national stations, and it has plans for another five new national services including a sport station to complement Radio 5 Live; a speech-based station with a mix of comedy, drama, stories and features and 'regular sections' devoted to children; a station that 'focuses on black music, news and speech aimed at a young audience'; a station focusing on music from the 1970s to the 1990s; and a national Asian station.[1]

The national commercial service, Digital One, went on air in November 1999. This is owned by a consortium including the GWR group, who are the major shareholders and own the national station Classic FM, and National Transcommunications Ltd (NTL), the telecommunications company that also runs the transmitter network for commercial radio. Through its multiplex it broadcasts the existing national analogue stations Classic FM, Virgin Radio and talkSPORT. But like the BBC, commercial broadcasters realise that the replication of existing services is not enough to tempt consumers to buy digital receivers so they have five other services broadcasting exclusively on digital radio. This comprises three different music stations; a station aimed at 'older listeners'; a speech-based station, Oneword, that focuses on plays, books, comedy and reviews; a rolling news station, ITN News; and one that deals with finance and business news.

In the same way that the BBC has control of its own analogue transmitters, and the Radio Authority controls those used by the independent sector, the BBC has control of its own national multiplex, while the Radio Authority controls the national commercial multiplex and the first licence was awarded for 12 years.[2]

At a regional and local level, however, the situation is slightly different. The Radio Authority is in charge of licensing all regional and local multiplexes, and the licensee then contracts with the BBC to provide a local service within the multiplex. This means, for example, that the two multiplexes currently serving Scotland that are both owned by Group Scottish Radio Holdings plc, who own Edinburgh's Forth FM and Glasgow's Clyde 1 FM, also carry BBC Radio Scotland as one of its services.

However, for all its perceived benefits digital radio has two interlinked drawbacks. The first is that in order to receive the service consumers have to invest in new radio sets. The initial cost of these was prohibitively high, making audiences for the new stations almost non-existent in the early years. Since 2000 the price of the sets has fallen, and many top-of-the-range new cars are now fitted with digital radios. It is also possible to buy a special card for PCs for as little as £100 that will allow the service to be played through computers. Nonetheless, most commentators believe it will be 2010 before the majority of the population has access to digital radio.

The second drawback is that the start-up costs involved make launching into digital broadcasting impossible for all but the big players in radio. A glance at the existing licences awarded for local multiplexes shows that every one has gone to one of the existing big radio groups including GWR, Capital, Emap, and Group Scottish Radio Holdings.

Of course the Radio Authority would counteract that, although small operators might not be able to own the licence for a multiplex, there is nothing to stop them running a service as part of one. The licences are not awarded to the highest cash bidder, but considered on merit, and among the criteria for local applications, the Radio Authority requires applicants to show:

- To what extent the radio services proposed by applicants appeal to a variety of local tastes and interests. The legislation also requires a broadening of local digital choice to be taken into account.

- How fair applicants have been in contracting with providers of radio programmes and data services who wish to be included in the multiplex.

(Radio Authority Fact Sheet Number Four)

Moreover, in order to make DAB more attractive to existing stations, any analogue service that broadcasts on a digital multiplex has its analogue licence automatically extended for a further eight years.

But the stark reality is that until digital radio audiences grow, it will not produce enough revenue to be self-financing, and by the time it does those stations in at the beginning will be firmly entrenched. For radio operators like Don Kotak, the managing director of a small independent station in Leicester, this means digital radio will be in the hands of a few large operators. 'The problem we have – while nobody will admit it – is that all the digital areas are being carved up by the big companies among themselves and it will cost anybody else who wants to provide a service up to £90,000 a year,' he says. 'That's fine – but we're not going to generate that revenue. All the research shows it will be 2010 before it is commonly used, so from now until then you're faced with huge expenditure with no return. The large companies have to go with it because they've got a different agenda – it's an investment in the future – but we can't do that.'

Nonetheless for digital radio to succeed it has to offer more than the current services in better-quality sound, and to some extent, at least for the time being, that should ensure that whoever provides the service it will have more diverse programming than the analogue services.

Internet radio

Radio on the Internet, or webcasting as it is known, is a growing phenomenon with literally thousands of radio stations across the world available through computer modems. Its supporters claim that it is a new medium that removes the barriers to entry out of radio broadcasting because it is not dependent on regulated licences and is relatively cheap to set up. Its detractors, however, point out that, like other aspects of the Internet, it is unregulated and uncontrolled and can encourage music piracy because music can be downloaded on to CD for future use.

However, radio and the Internet appear to complement each other very well and all the major stations in Britain as well as many smaller stations now have web sites. As mentioned in the previous chapter, one of the main factors behind the increase in radio listening is that people tune in, either to conventional radio or through the Internet, while they are working on their computers.

But Internet radio sites are not just about listening to a station's live output via computer. The sites also provide background information about programmes and presenters, allow users to access travel information and news, provide 'virtual' tours of the station, and give them a direct link to programmes through email. Indeed as PC penetration in homes grows, and the cost of accessing the Internet falls, programmes as diverse as the *Steve Penk Breakfast Show* on Virgin Radio and the *Today* programme on BBC Radio 4 increasingly refer and respond to listeners' emails they have just received.

The BBC has a web site for each of its national and local services available at BBC Online where, as well as providing information about programmes and presenters, selected excerpts can be listened to and there are links to other web sites of interest.

Although slower off the mark than the BBC, the big commercial groups are also keen to establish an on-line presence, and both Capital Radio and the GWR group launched their sites at the end of 2000, keen to exploit a market that allows advertisers to reach an audience 'simultaneously over the airwaves and on screen' (Mills 2000).

But Internet radio is not just confined to existing stations going on-line. In June 2000 stormlive.com, the 'UK's first Internet radio station to broadcast live 24 hours-a-day', was launched with the slogan 'the future has no frequency'. As well as having its own site, the 'virtual station' also broadcasts over the Freeserve Internet service provider channel bringing with it a whole new vocabulary. The presenters are called EJs rather than DJs, and those connected to the service are referred to as 'streamies' because of the streaming technology involved in bringing audio to a computer (Court 2000).

Radio on the Internet can also play an important role in keeping channels of communication open in areas under the control of a repressive regime. This was most notably demonstrated during the uprisings in Serbia in 1996, when the then Yugoslav President Slobodan Milosevic tried to stop the broadcasting of reports by the independent Serbian radio station Radio B-92 about anti-government demonstrations over the annulment of municipal elections. After the station's transmitter was switched off, the station posted print versions of its news on its web site, and also began using RealAudio to broadcast on-line, reaching people not only in Yugoslavia but equally importantly all over the world (Fleming 2000).

Even in democracies the Internet allows access to broadcasting by groups previously restricted. As Stephen Barnard points out, 'Pirate radio operators have found they can broadcast freely, without interruption or fear of prosecution, via the Internet' (2000: 253). And increasingly student radio is going on-line to avoid the high cost of RSL licences and transmitter costs.

But Internet radio has its drawbacks. In Britain and many other countries where going on-line is charged at the local telephone call rate it is an expensive way to listen to a 'free' service. And although the number of households on-line is growing, very few people have Internet access compared to those who have radios. It is also dependent on a computer and connection to a telephone line and for the time being that makes it less portable than traditional radio. That said, in the USA there is already a product available that looks like a conventional radio but plugs into a telephone socket and plays Internet radio (Court 2000) so technological advances could soon manage to overcome these problems.

Satellite and cable radio

The problem of portability is also shared by satellite and cable radio because sets have to be connected to either a dish or cable network. In most cases the services available via satellite or cable are those already available on analogue or digital terrestrial radio. All the national BBC services plus the BBC World Service are available via the Astra satellite, as is Virgin Radio and the London Asian station Sunrise. Cable radio which broadcasts over a local cable network is less prevalent and tends to be used by community radio stations, although a series of music-based stations each dealing with a different genre (chart, rock, indie, jazz, etc.) is available in London.

The main advantage of satellite broadcasting is that it can be accessed from anywhere, and this is of particular use for stores who want to have their own radio station playing in all their branches like Homebase FM and Costcutter Radio. It is also used to provide a service to other broadcasters. The Student Broadcast Network, for example, provides programmes like the student Radio Chart show on its satellite service, which can then be relayed through various student radio stations across the country. On a larger scale, the World Radio Network provides programmes from 20 different public service broadcasters across the world. These can be heard directly via satellite, but they are also available for small stations to rebroadcast on AM or FM for the cost of downlinking the material from satellite.

Hospital radio

Hospital radio began in the 1920s to 'help relieve the boredom and isolation a period of hospitalisation causes'.[3] It now has over 300 individual stations that broadcast mainly through a closed-circuit system accessed through bedside headphones, although some broadcast on low power AM or FM transmitters. The service is run entirely by volunteers, loosely overseen by the Hospital Broadcasting Association, a national charity that provides technical and programming advice and promotes the services.

The aim of the service is to 'ensure the patient is kept in touch with their local community, family and friends in a way no other broadcasting medium can attain'. And while the service is acknowledged by the Department of Health as beneficial to patients, most hospital radio stations have to raise their own funds to maintain their service.

However, hospital radio also has another often unacknowledged role in that it is a valuable training ground for up-and-coming radio presenters. Many current radio personalities began their career as one of the 11,500 hospital radio volunteers, and it is still used as a pool of potential talent by radio station managers on the look-out for new presenters.

Pirate radio

Pirate radio – unlicensed illegal broadcasting – was at its height in Britain in the 1960s and enjoyed another surge of interest in the 1980s. Nowadays pirate radio is usually referred to as 'non-licensed radio', although licensed broadcasters tend to use the term 'unlicensed radio'. The first British pirate station was Radio Caroline which began broadcasting from a ship off the coast of Essex in March 1964. By 1968 21 pirate stations were broadcasting with an estimated total daily audience of between 10 and 15 million (Shingler and Wieringa 1998: 24).

This first wave of pirate broadcasters were unashamedly commercial in their output, influenced by the format of Radio Luxembourg and American radio stations. Most followed a top-40 music format with casual, chatty links from DJs so that in both style and content the stations were the antithesis of BBC broadcasting at the time. It is generally acknowledged that the restructuring of BBC radio with the creation of BBC Radios 1, 2, 3 and 4 in 1967 was a reaction to the popularity of pirate radio, and Andrew Crisell believes they also inspired the creation of local radio.

> First they were in some sense 'local' themselves. None of them broadcast over an area larger than the Home Counties, many of them publicised local events and aroused local loyalties, and a few such as Radio London and Radio Essex took local names. Second, although they afforded no broadcasting access to actual members of the public, they broke the BBC's virtual monopoly of radio to fulfil a demand which it had neglected, and so in that sense assumed a 'public' voice.
>
> (Crisell 1994: 33)

However, despite the creation of Radio 1 – whose first DJs often came from pirate stations – and the 1967 Marine Broadcasting (Offences) Act which officially outlawed the stations, pirate radio continued, moving from ships and sea-based platforms to urban areas in the 1970s. As Shingler and Wieringa point out, 'During the 1980s growth in terrestrial pirates was so massive that at one stage illegal operators actually outnumbered legal broadcasters' (1998: 25).

Throughout this period pirate stations met with increasing opposition, especially from the BBC. They claimed that the pirate stations caused interference on legitimate services and could interfere with frequencies used by the emergency services. They also objected that the pirate stations did not pay royalties on the music they played, and this could have an adverse effect on the music industry. Nonetheless the pirate stations like Radio Invicta, JFM, and London Weekend Radio continued to gain audiences and increasingly operated quite openly. As well as catering to marginalised music communities ignored by mainstream broadcasters – such as reggae, hip-hop, jazz, rhythm and blues – they also catered to ethnic minorities through stations like London Greek Radio which broadcast to the Greek and Greek Cypriot communities.

The demise of pirate radio came about with the 1990 Broadcast Act which opened up the development of commercial radio to try to encourage diversity in radio. As a result, many pirates like London's dance-music station Kiss FM applied for licences to the new Radio Authority and went legitimate. However, since then the number of unlicensed broadcasts appears to have increased, in part because many non-licensed broadcasters feel let down by the 1990 Act, believing the changes it brought about have undermined community-orientated stations and small-scale radio entrepreneurs.

In an effort to stop non-licensed broadcasting, operators are heavily fined if they are caught and can even face a prison sentence.[4] Moreover, further legal action may be taken by the 'official' stations in the non-licensed broadcasting area. In summer 2000 the Commercial Radio Companies Association (CRCA) initiated legal action against Scene FM who broadcast dance music at weekends until they were closed down in 1998. In the first case of its kind, the CRCA sued the pirate station for £50,000 for causing interference to transmissions and a reduction in advertising revenue.

Community radio[5]

The chief characteristics of community radio are that it is participatory – being run by those who also make up its audience – and that it is non-profit-making. This does not mean that it eschews advertising, but that all profits are put back into the running of the station which is owned and run by the community it broadcasts to. As one definition explains:

> It should be made clear that community radio is not about doing something for the community but about the community doing something for itself, i.e. owning and controlling its own means of communication.
>
> (AMARC web site)

In Britain community radio has been slow to develop compared to other parts of the world. The Community Media Association (CMA), which was formerly the Community Radio Association, argues that specific legislation is needed to aid the development of community services. They point to the example of community radio in France, which has a separate licence category to provide protection from takeovers by networks and for-profit organisations, and a special fund based on a levy on the advertising revenue of commercial broadcasters provides revenue to support the stations.

It had been hoped that the 1990 Broadcasting Act would lead to a growth in community radio stations but according to CMA director Steve Buckley this has not happened because of the economics of radio broadcasting whereby small stations are bought out for their licences. As Buckley comments,

> This severely distorts the market since licences are acquired on merit but sold to the highest bidder. This economy is a deterrent to public and community investment in small-scale services. Public agencies and charitable donors do not want to invest in local community projects if this is seen to be taken for private profit. A separate licensing category is therefore an essential underpinning of their economic viability.
>
> (*Airflash*, issue 69: 21)

What the CMA and other organisations including the Radio Authority want is a third tier of broadcasting to operate in a complementary way to existing BBC and commercial radio, with separate licensing and regulation to protect it. Currently full-time community radio services mainly operate in remote rural areas like Radio Ceredigion in West Wales, and Oban Fm and Nevis Radio in the Highlands and Islands. Other community radio services operate on RSLs normally limited to 28 days. Through the CMA these small-scale stations receive advice and training and are kept informed through conferences organised by the CMA and a quarterly magazine, *Airflash*. Since 1997 the remit of the CRA has extended to cover all forms of community media including radio, television, cable and Internet broadcasting. But according to Steve Buckley radio is still the most appropriate medium for community access to the means of communication which is regarded as a vital component of democracy. As he explains,

> It provides a local counterbalance to media concentration and globalisation. It provides a route into new information and communication

technologies based on creative work and creative content. It provides access to those most in danger of exclusion from this new economy.

(*Airflash*, issue 69: 21)

Community radio is also important as a training ground for new entrants to radio, and as a place where new ideas can be tried. This is especially relevant at a time when in-house training by ILR and the BBC is being cut back, and when format radio is increasingly being adopted. As the CRCA note, 'These operations [community radio services] bring valuable new talent into our sector . . . creative industries rely upon the fostering of new ideas and talent for their creative renewal' (*Airflash*, issue 69: 13).

With so much support for a third tier of broadcasting, as well as the availability of digital frequencies that in the long term might free space on analogue frequencies, the future of community radio in Britain looks better than at any time in its history.

Restricted Service Licences

Restricted Service Licences (RSLs) are temporary licences granted by the Radio Authority to operate on a low-power basis for a limited geographical area, typically to cover a town or a 3-kilometre radius in a city. Most licences are granted for a maximum of 28 days, and outside London groups can apply for two RSL licences a year as long as there is a four-month gap between the two services.

RSLs are used for two different purposes. The most common one is to cover special events, like an agricultural show or bigger events like the Edinburgh Festival, or for charity fund-raising by a local community, as in the Radio Cracker broadcasts around Christmas in many towns. As previously mentioned they are also used by community groups who want to provide a highly localised service, or by ethnic minority groups who do not feel fully represented by mainstream radio.

The second use of RSLs is as a trial run for a proposed permanent service, to demonstrate the need for a service in that particular area and gauge support for it. As shown in the profile of Oak FM in Chapter 1, this information can then be used to back up an application for a full-time licence, but the Radio Authority make it clear that an RSL does not guarantee that they will advertise a full-term licence.

The Radio Authority also issues long-term restricted service licences (LRSLs) for radio stations to serve a single establishment like a hospital or university campus. To qualify for an LRSL the establishment concerned must have a permanent member of staff to be the licence holder, and meet the RA's legal and technical requirements. Licences are granted for a maximum of five years and are automatically renewable. In October 2000 there were 79 LRSLs operating, mainly in universities and hospitals, but also on army and airforce bases.

RSLs are not cheap. Each application incurs a £200 fee which is normally not refundable if the application is rejected, unless it is because there is not a suitable frequency available. On top of this a tariff is charged for every day of the licence, including any time used for testing and any days when there is no broadcasting. The tariff varies according to whether it is an AM or FM frequency and the strength of the signal,[6] and must be paid before the licence is issued. Added to this is the cost of renting the use of a transmitter that is usually more than the total cost of the licence.

Generally RSLs are issued on a first-come-first-served basis, but applications must be received at least six weeks before the proposed service goes on air, and will not be considered more than a year in advance. Usually only one RSL is permitted in any area at the same time, with a gap between the ending of one RSL and the beginning of another. There are also restrictions for RSLs in areas where there are plans to advertise a full local radio licence or readvertise an existing one.

Under the 1990 Broadcasting Act certain groups and individuals are automatically disqualified from holding an RSL including local authorities and political groups. However, local authorities can usually fund an RSL, and political organisations may fund one as long as the Radio Authority is 'satisfied it is not against public interest'. Similarly, religious groups can hold a licence as long as they 'do not practise or advocate illegal behaviour or have rites or other forms of collective observance that are not normally directly accessible to the general public' (RSLs: Notes for Applicants: 18).

Despite the bureaucracy and expense involved in an RSL they are very popular. As the profiles below show, RSLs are used for a variety of reasons by a wide range of people but at their core is the ability they have to provide an identity to specific groups who feel their needs are not being met by mainstream radio as well as providing those interested in radio with hands-on experience.

Profile

Profile Fly FM
Radio for students by students

The Nottingham Trent University first began broadcasting in 1996 when its Students' Union decided a radio station would complement the student newspaper, *Platform*, and add to their entertainment programme. As SU general manager Sylvia Whalton explains, the university helped fund the station's first year, matching the SU's investment of £25,000 to help equip purpose-built studios in the Student Union building, and pay for a full-time station manager. 'We had a full time manager for four years,' Sylvia explains. 'This was to give us continuity between the RSLs and, because we were new to this field, to give us some assurances about what was being broadcast and that the equipment was being handled properly.'

In its first four years of broadcasting twice a year, in November and April, the station has gone through several changes. The first big one came after two years when the station – then called Kick FM – was forced to change its name because another station had a copyright on it. That called for a relaunch and a change of name to Fly FM.

Another blow came two years later when the expected April RSL was given to a commercial station wanting to do a trial run as a regional dance-music station, followed by the resignation of the station manager. The future of the station was in doubt.

One of the reasons behind employing a full-time manager was to meet the Radio Authority's requirements for a permanent member of staff needed to get an LRSL, but when it was realised that it was unlikely the station would manage to be permanent it was decided to change tactics. 'We were at a crossroads,' explains Sylvia Whalton. 'In the end we decided to keep the budget to a minimum and use what we've invested to give the students hands-on experience of radio.'

The station budget is around £15,000 a year with each licence costing around £1,000 and between £2,500–£3,000 needed to pay for renting the transmitter. Another expense is indemnity insurance which the SU take out in case the station gets sued. 'We've had nine RSLs now and never had any trouble but it's still something you need,' says Sylvia.

The student management team comprises a station manager, assistant manager, programme controller, head of music, head of production, head of sales and head of promotions. The manager for 2000/01 was third-year international relations student, Katrina Gill, who started working with the management team in July towards the November RSL, to be ready with a new station logo at the beginning of term.

Katrina explains that each head of department has responsibility for training their team in a specific area. The assistant manager, who covers for Katrina while she is in lectures, is in charge of DJs and works with the programme controller and head of music on the station's format. The head of productions makes all the station's jingles and adverts, liaising with the heads of sales and promotions to get firms interested in backing the station.

As well as the usual flyers and adverts in the university, the station is promoted through the student newspaper and its output is piped directly to the Student Union bar.

'The hardest part is organising everything and getting people to come to meetings,' says Katrina. 'Because they're students and this isn't their main job you have to recognise that and not put too much pressure on them. They're volunteers and you have to recognise that and get the right balance.' The station follows a traditional format with a breakfast show, mid-morning show, lunch-time show, afternoon show and drive-time that work from an agreed playlist of contemporary music. After 7 p.m. it goes to more specialist music. 'We've got a broad mix of music from drum and bass, rock, R&B right through to jazz and blues,' says Katrina. 'We do promote student activities but we're a community station and we like to include the community and cover cultural events like cinema and theatre reviews.'

The station is helped by having a broadcast journalism degree at the university, whose students provide hourly news, features and sport throughout the day and at weekends. 'The standard of the news provided is excellent,' says Katrina. 'I've spoken to a lot of other student stations who wish they had something like that – and it obviously helps the broadcast journalism department by giving students hands-on experience.' Her aim is to get every department in the university to contribute to the station. 'We've got a lot of departments with a lot of talent who can all contribute,' she says.

The station is also given help by the Student Radio Association. As well as providing training sessions at conferences, the SRA is a way for student broadcasters to meet each other and those working in the industry. They also have regional representatives who can be contacted if there are any legal issues that need to be checked, and their web site has useful help-sheets with technical and presentation tips.

Although hard work, Katrina says there is no shortage of volunteers to work on all aspects of the station. 'I think initially people get involved because they think of it as something new and interesting and then they realise that there could be jobs in it and it's being taken seriously by the industry,' she says. Katrina's own experience has shown how valuable working on the student station can be in getting paid work. As a result of presenting the Breakfast Show on Fly, she was given the chance to take part in a Radio 1 campaign about student debt, and broadcast live on the Sunday afternoon Sarah Cox Show. An offer of summer work from Channel 9 in Northern Ireland followed, and she has since secured a place with an Australian broadcasting company for when she graduates.

'It is pretty stressful when it's 24 hours a day but everyone's very enthusiastic and it's great fun,' she says. The station has won several Radio 1 Student Radio Awards and that encourages everyone to keep standards high, but Katrina says the most important part of Fly FM is that it delivers a service to students.

'We don't want to be the best radio station,' she explains, 'we want to be the best *student* radio station – that's a station run by students for students.'

Profile | Radio Ramzan
Radio to communicate and educate

Running a radio station with the backing of a large university and Student Union is quite different from starting from scratch in a deprived inner-city area, as Fazal Malik well knows. But as with the student station, it has its rewards. 'It's the feedback from the community that keeps us going,' says the inner-city community worker.

The Nottingham station started in 1997 as a way to help address problems with health, housing, employment, crime and low achievement in education. Like other Radio Ramzans in cities like Bradford, London, Leeds and Glasgow, the station broadcasts over the fasting month of Ramadan. 'One of the reasons for the station's success is that we do it around Ramadan when people are fasting and go to mosque more and think more of charity,' Fazal explains. 'The station is not purely religious, however, we also have programmes on education, training and development and culture. Unlike other Radio Ramzans we also play music.'

The station is funded in part by organisations like the Karimia Institute which is a mosque and a cultural centre, the Pakistani Centre and health organisations in the city, as well as small businesses in the Asian community. 'From the beginning small businesses have supported us – like the butcher shop, small corner shops, take-aways and taxi firms,' says Fazal. 'These are the people who listen to us and support us – we must have invested five or six thousand pounds given by them over the last three years.'

The station's studios are in a rented house in the heart of Nottingham's Asian district and that means they have to be made from scratch every year. For the first three years the station also had to hire equipment every year, but slowly they have managed to buy pieces so that now they are virtually fully self-equipped and have even bought their own transmitter to save on renting one. The permanent equipment will also be able to be used to train people before the station goes on air.

'I had some background in radio because I have a degree from City University and radio was one of the things I studied,' Fazal explains. 'But doing it in practice is quite different and I had to learn as I went along and we made some terrible mistakes in the beginning.' But Fazal does not think this detracts from the station's appeal. 'People like it because it's not like BBC radio which is highly professional and slick,' he says. 'We make mistakes and people understand that it's their own people from their own community.'

Almost 6 per cent of Nottingham's population belong to an ethnic minority group with the largest South Asian group being Pakistani Muslims mainly from the Mirpuri district of Kashmir. They speak Mirpuri Punjabi which is a regional dialect with no written script, and literacy levels in both English and Urdu (the main language of Pakistan) are low especially in women and the elderly. Because of this Radio Ramzan broadcasts in a mixture of languages – English and Urdu as well as Mirpuri and Bengali.

The station has a mix of programmes designed to appeal to a wide age group. It starts at 6 a.m. when fasting begins and the daytime programmes concentrate on women and the elderly. Late afternoon there is a quiz programme for school children and in the early evening there are music and cultural programmes aimed at younger people.

Among the most popular shows are health programmes made in association with health care groups in Nottingham. 'The interpretation of our health messages within an Islamic perspective added authority to what we were saying and increased the chances that listeners would take notice of what was being said,' explains Roger Williams, the chief executive of the City Centre Primary Care Group who are involved with the station. 'Radio is a brilliant medium for helping us to do this. It is immediate, you can talk to people in their own homes and get feedback from listeners to the messages we are giving out.'

Interactivity is an important part of the whole RSL and the station has two lines into the studio for people to go on air directly or leave messages with the reception to be read out later.

Programmes on religious and political issues are also popular and studio guests feature local councillors, Muslim MPs and even cricketer and politician Imran Khan talking from Islamabad. 'We get 200 or more calls for these programmes,' says Fazal. 'The response is phenomenal because we do what interests the local community.'

And the community's involvement with the station grows each year with elderly people in their 70s staffing the reception to take calls and see to studio guests, and younger people enthusiastic to make programmes. 'Some of them are so keen they want to make it their career – we've even got one volunteer who's taking 15 days off work to give us technical back-up,' says Fazal. 'We're hoping that through links with local colleges we'll be able to run proper courses for people who want to go into radio professionally.'

However, running the station has its problems. The RSL costs almost £2,500 a year because the station transmits on the highest power available in order to reach as much of the city as possible. And despite its popularity there is no guarantee that they will get a licence. 'We are very popular with our community but every year we have to go through the application not knowing if it's going to be awarded or go to some other group,' Fazal explains.

Fazal believes the radio station has not only helped the Muslim community in a direct way by providing them with important information on health, education and employment, but also indirectly by giving them self-confidence and a clear identity – something the mainstream media do not do.

'The problem with the BBC Asian Network, for example, is that it is still too general. They categorise Asians as one monolithic, homogeneous community which is just not true,' he explains. 'They [ethnic minorities] are already marginalised in society and mainstream media don't cater to their needs so they are further marginalised. Under these circumstances community media have a positive role to integrate them into society and provide a platform to plead and propagate their own issues.'

Although Fazal believes the station is both needed and wanted by the Asian community, he also recognises that it will never be able to become a permanent service. 'There is a need and I know we could do it but the cost of the licence fee is a big problem,' he laments. 'I can't understand why Britain does not do more for community radio. There is very good community radio in Australia, South America and Canada and even our neighbours in France and Germany have a good system. It's time Britain did more for community radio.'

Notes

1   Taken from 'Digital Radio – New Services' at www.bbc.co.uk, October 2000.
2   For a fuller discussion of the role of the Radio Authority in commercial radio see Chapter 9.
3   Information from the Hospital Broadcasting Association web site at www.hbauk. com.
4   In June 2000 two defendants were sentenced to four and six months in prison at Southend Crown Court, for operating a pirate radio station that caused interference to Rochester Airport air traffic control. Quoted in *Airflash*, issue 69.
5   See Chapter 9 for more details of proposals for 'access radio' made in the Communications White Paper 2000.
6   Full details are available in the Radio Authority's *RSLs: Notes for Applicants*. In 2000 the fees ranged from £28 a day for AM, to £80 a day for FM broadcasts above 1W.

3 Radio style

....

very radio station strives to achieve an identifiable style. Although the style may be similar to others within the same group – for example, BBC local radio or all Emap stations – every station wants to be heard as offering an identifiable product that is different from other stations available in the area. The most obvious way a station declares its identity is through its choice of music (or lack of it) and the style of its presenters. But the identity of a station is also detectable in the station's jingles, its logo, the kind of competitions it runs, and all its promotional material, as will be examined in more detail later in this chapter. In other words, the radio station is more than just its output. It is a set of attitudes and values that constitute its brand.

The branding of radio stations and its importance within the industry reflect the increasing commodification of radio. Radio is not just a form of information and entertainment, it is a 'product' to be consumed by the audience. As with other products it has to fulfil certain basic requirements of the consumer. For example in choosing which supermarket we shop in the basic requirement is that it stocks food and drink. The basic requirement we have for a radio station is that it provides information and entertainment. Beyond that, however, the brand we choose also says something about what is important to us: someone who shops in Costcutter is more likely to be interested in the prices of the goods than someone who shops in Sainsbury's where the price is less important than the perceived quality of the goods. Similarly listeners to BBC 5 Live are more likely to be interested in news and sport than listeners to Classic FM whose taste is for light classical music. And just as supermarket shoppers can be won or lost by a range of features that have nothing to do with the basic service they provide – such as the quality of their trolleys or carrier bags or the attitude of the check-out staff – so too can radio listeners be won or lost by details like the frequency and style of their jingles or the comments of a particular presenter.

Branding, then, is a way of achieving a consistent identity for the radio station that is delivered through every part of its programming and promotions. As Steve Orchard, the GWR group programme director says, 'A strong brand is without doubt one of the most valuable assets any business can have. For us a brand is about much more than the mix of music we play – or the contests we run. It's about understanding the deep-seated reasons people listen to us – and nurturing a powerful, lasting relationship with them.'[1]

In other words, giving a radio station an identifiable brand encourages listener loyalty: we want to be associated with a particular station because it has an image we like. This chapter looks at the way radio stations achieve their brand identity, but before doing so it considers something all stations work around – the radio day.

The radio day

Radio output is not just a random selection of programmes or segments but a carefully considered blend of audio designed with a particular audience in mind in a way that will meet the audience's basic requirement for information and entertainment without them switching off. To achieve this radio stations attempt to match the pace, style and content of their programmes to the daily routines of their listeners. In other words radio tries to complement the real-life activities of listeners with content that suits their needs and moods at a particular time of day, while at the same time providing a schedule that appears new every day and at the same time has a routine that is 'natural'. As Paddy Scannell observes,

> The effect of the temporal arrangements of radio and television is such as to pick out each day as *this* day, this day in particular, this day as its *own* day, caught up in its own immediacy with its own involvements and concerns. The huge investment of labour (care) that goes to produce the output of broadcasting delivers a service whose most generalizable effect is to re-temporise time.
>
> (1996: 149)

To achieve this, broadcasters break the day into segments, or what Scannell calls 'zones', that match the daily life of most people, making the programmes 'appropriate to who in particular is available to listen at what time and in what circumstances' (1996: 150).

The breakfast show

The most important programme on any radio station is its breakfast show. This is the time when most people listen to the radio, and as the station's flagship programme, it is used for a number of different purposes, the most obvious being to hook listeners into the station, hopefully for the rest of the day. The breakfast show also establishes the station's identity or brand – whether it is a BBC or commercial station, national or local, speech- or music-based, and what style of music it broadcasts. This is done not only through the content of the actual show but also by 'trailing' programmes scheduled for later in the day. The idea is to keep the audience coming back for more. One GWR station, for example, featured a 'joke of the day' in its breakfast show omitting the punch line. Listeners then phoned in throughout the day with suggested punch lines before the real one was delivered towards the end of the drive-time show. Other stations use competitions to keep their listeners tuned in throughout the day. For example, Virgin Radio ran a competition that involved listeners being able to list the name of the song and the artist for an hour-long 'ten songs in a row' sequence to win £1,000.

As the managing director of Leicester Sound, Phil Dixon, explains, the radio day has a predictable pattern that broadcasters have to try to exploit. 'You peak during breakfast-time then the audience reduces throughout the day, picking up a bit at drive-time with people coming home from work and it tails off again in the evening,' he says.[2] 'We try to encourage people to listen for as long as possible and keep listening throughout the day.'

According to the GWR group, the breakfast show is:

A lynchpin to the station's output, the local breakfast show sets the tone and personality for the station as a whole. It's a dynamic and enter-taining start to the day that gets you out of bed and out to work – brim-ming with great music, stacks of listener interaction, entertainment and all the local and national info you need. Valuable social ammunition.

(GWR brand document)

Many breakfast shows, whether speech- or music-based, are done by a 'team' of presenters who each have a distinctive on-air personality. The main presenters on Radio 4's *Today* programme, for example, each have a different style of interviewing. John Humphrys is known for his aggressive, almost bullying approach, while the no less tenacious James Naughtie has a more paternalistic, reasoned way of dealing with interviewees that balances the programme.

As Phil Dixon explains, the idea behind a breakfast team on GWR stations is to have a set of people with distinctive roles that will appeal to the different characteristics of the audience. 'We like to think of our breakfast shows as a group of friends having fun and if you look at programmes like *The Simpsons*, *Friends*, or *Frazier* they're very successful because they have specific character roles in their programmes and we try to copy that,' he says.

> We need to have an anchor who is someone who carries out all the benchmarks we have as a radio station like time-checks, travel and the music, and is warm and approachable. Then we have a picture painter – a storyteller – what we call the 'innocent fool', although the word 'fool' is a bit misleading – it's just that things happen to them. They come in on Monday morning and say 'you'll never guess what happened to me at the weekend . . .' Then the third character is the scatter-brained stunt boy – someone who's a bit younger than the others – a bit cocky, a bit cheeky, but still warm, approachable and likeable. The one thing we don't want is anyone who offends the audience. Everybody has to be likeable but they've each got to have their own distinctive characteristics.

Irrespective of the type of programme it is, the breakfast show nearly always features regular time-checks to keep people on course for getting out of the house, traffic and travel news to help them plan their journeys, and news of what has happened overnight as well as what is likely to happen in the rest of the day. It is generally assumed that most of the audience tunes in for around 20 minutes, so a certain amount of repetition is allowed, especially on important news stories or particularly 'hot' show-biz gossip.

Daytime shows

The pace of programmes tends to slow down a little after the breakfast show as it is assumed most people are where they are going to be for the rest of the day by 9 or 10 a.m. Traditionally this zone of broadcasting was aimed at housewives, but it is now recognised that daytime radio is used by a wide variety of people either at work or travelling, as well as those at home. According to Jane Hill of the Lincs FM group, daytime radio is about connecting with the audience wherever they are and should give the impression that 'we're all here together'.

Generally, daytime programming assumes a slightly more focused listener and tends to feature competitions, requests, particularly in the lunchtime segment, and phone-ins like Nicky Campbell's topical news phone-in on BBC 5 Live. The idea behind them is to provide what one listener described as 'chewing gum for the brain' (Hargrave 2000: 12) – something to keep people involved and interested without too much effort.

Drive-time shows

The pace picks up again on most stations as the traditional working day comes to an end. Drive-time shows serve the same function as breakfast shows but in reverse. Their job is to provide information about traffic and travel to get people home from work, as well as news about what has happened during the day. Just as the breakfast show trails programmes on the station later in the day, drive-time acts as a bridge between daytime programmes and those on later in the evening.

Evening and overnight shows

The audience for radio generally after 7 p.m. is very small mainly because television is the primary form of home entertainment. Traditionally it is in the evening that less mainstream programmes are aired. Often these are specialist music shows featuring country, jazz, dance or alternative music, but often this is the time when broadcasts for ethnic minorities are aired in what has been dubbed the 'conscience slot'. The thinking behind this is that if you have a 'minority' interest you will make the effort to hear these programmes, and if you do not you will most likely not be listening at that time anyway.

Ironically, evening and night broadcasting is often more innovative than that of the daytime, as John Peel has shown since the early days of Radio 1 when he established a cult following by introducing alternative music to listeners. It is seen as a time when new formats can be tested and new presenters tried out particularly on smaller stations. Many mainstream presenters start their careers on late-night shows, like James Whale whose controversial phone-in style was first used on Metro Radio in Newcastle in the early 1980s between 11 p.m. and 2 a.m.

DJ Joanna Russell (see Profile: Chapter 4) says she loved doing the overnight show on Minster FM in York partly because it gave her more freedom than a daytime show, but mainly because of the reaction of the audience. 'People who are listening overnight are actually really listening,' she explains. 'They're not running around and just catching a few seconds of what you say – they actually really focus. If they're by themselves they're glad that you're there and you get loads of phone calls which is really nice.'

Nonetheless night-time radio tends to be overlooked by station managers, with many using pre-recorded or group networked shows to fill the slot to save money. After 7 p.m. many BBC local stations broadcast on a regional basis, and the entire service switches to BBC 5 Live between midnight and 5 a.m.

Weekend shows

Weekend programmes reflect the fact that for most people this is leisure time so they tend to be more relaxed whatever the style of the station. Traditionally, sport features prominently on Saturday afternoons although this is done in different ways.

Predictably, stations like talkSPORT and BBC 5 Live devote their entire Saturday afternoon to sport but many music-based stations feature match reports and goal updates during the football season (see Chapter 7 for more details about sports programming). Virgin Radio, for example, features a lunch-time phone-in with football expert Terry Venables who answers calls between records, followed by a 'zoo' format programme headed by Chris Evans which provides match reports and interrupts the music every time a goal is scored anywhere in the country. Local radio also features sport heavily on a Saturday afternoon often providing commentary on local teams with regular updates from other key games.

For many stations, then, the weekend audience, particularly on a Saturday afternoon, is slightly different from their weekday one, and as BBC editor Kate Squire explains, that is a chance to 'sell' the station to a wider audience. 'We get a lot of younger men who tune in on a Saturday afternoon who listen to no other part of our output,' she says. 'The trick is to try to hook them in so we play a lot of trails or talk about other programmes they might be interested in to try to carry them over.'[3]

Other stations, however, recognise that their attraction on Saturday afternoon is that they provide an escape from sport. 'Sport is relevant to our listeners but it's not the big thing some people make it out to be,' says Phil Dixon of Leicester Sound. 'We give our audience sports headline news and since we stopped doing match reports our audience on a Saturday afternoon has virtually doubled.'

But no matter what radio style a station has, its day follows a predictable pattern that mirrors the average life in its sequence and flow. Each station gives more or less significance to certain items but all work towards providing a meaningful structure to the day to the extent that for most of us a day without hearing the radio at all leaves us slightly disorientated. How we select which station to listen to is to some extent dependent on our needs. Someone needing to know about the latest developments in Sierra Leone is more likely to go to BBC Radio 4 than their local radio station, while someone needing to know about traffic delays in their area would do the reverse. But increasingly what attracts or repels listeners is the personality that the station projects, and this is done through carefully thought-out and deliberate branding, which we will now examine in more detail.

Branding a station

The branding of radio stations is about much more than their output and promotions: at root it is about what associations the audience make with the name of the station. As Jane Hill, the director of programming for the Lincs FM group points out, it is only since the mid-1990s that the branding of radio stations has become more of an issue. 'When commercial radio first started there was one local station and it was branded as that area's local station so there was no need to think carefully about it,' she says.[4] But the increasing number of services available in the same area mean stations now have to think carefully about the image they want to project.

'You need to think about the kind of people you're trying to appeal to. Not just the age group but the kind of interests they have and the kind of values they have and what you try to do is reflect those values in the programmes you put out, and think about every bit of promotional material as well,' Jane Hill explains. 'Your brand becomes something that's not quite what's on air and not quite what's seen – its quite amorphous.'

One of the reasons the branding of a radio station is difficult to define is that the product itself is intangible. As Pete Wilby and Andy Conroy observe, 'in a culture dominated by visual icons, radio operates on an experiential rather than tangible plain' (1994: 37). For this reason branding is done both on-air through the style of the presenters and programmes, and off-air through advertising and promotions that provide a visual representation of the station. As Jane Hill explains, the process is carried through every aspect of the station's contact with the audience often in subtle ways. 'We throw around words like "family values" and "trustworthiness",' she says. 'Now I would never want one of my presenters to go on air and say "your family-value station" or "your trustworthy station" but you make it so – by having competitions involving children, for example, or being first with all the local information people need. You take those areas of the brand values and then perhaps do a bus advertising campaign with a picture of a family and a friendly slogan, and then you go to events that involve your kind of audience, and you go to schools and give out sandwich bags and water bottles with the station logo on them. You have to follow the brand values all the way through.'

The BBC brand

Although technically the BBC is not a commercial broadcaster in that it is publicly funded, branding is still important to it for two main reasons. The first is that like all broadcasters the BBC needs to project an image of itself that will inspire loyalty in listeners. The second is that a strong brand image makes it easier for the corporation to sell its programmes abroad, earning money that can be used to supplement the licence fee.

The BBC brand is recognised worldwide as quality broadcasting. It is intimately linked to British society through its history and held up as an example of public service broadcasting that attracts audiences in large numbers, unlike other parts of the world, like America for example, where PSB is often unfairly associated with 'worthy but dull' programming.

From a marketing point of view, one reason the BBC is regarded so highly, especially at an international level, is that it constantly promotes the idea that it does not make programmes for profit but for the worthier motive of serving the public. This sense of being above market demands comes through in the BBC's statement of its editorial values:

> We aim to be the world's most creative and trusted broadcaster and pro-gramme maker, seeking to satisfy all our audiences with services that inform, educate and entertain and enrich their lives *in the ways that the market alone will not.* We aim to be guided by our public purposes; to encourage the UK's most innovative talents; *to act independently of all interests*, and to aspire to the highest ethical standards.
>
> (BBC Producers' Guidelines, emphasis added)[5]

This is not to suggest that the BBC does not deliver what it promises: as previously mentioned the BBC provides a greater range of radio programmes than any other British broadcaster. But it is interesting to note that as competition in radio in Britain increases, the BBC is taking an increasingly commercial approach to marketing itself by exploiting its unique selling point as *the* public service broadcaster in Britain, much to the annoyance of commercial radio who regard themselves as providing as much of a public service as they do.

The BBC also has an advantage over commercial broadcasters in the way it can, and does, promote its services through all of its outlets: the only advertisements on the BBC are for other BBC products. Increasingly BBC television features slickly produced adverts for BBC radio, BBC On-line and the BBC's digital services. However, as Baroness Young, the vice-chairman of the BBC board of governors, told an audience at the Radio Academy Radio Festival in Cardiff in 1999, the Corporation has a duty to tell the public about its services in whatever way it can. 'The commercial sector cries "foul" that we cross-promote radio programmes between different networks and on TV,' she said. 'We would be failing in our duty if we didn't! We must let the Radio 4 drama audience know that there is longer drama on Radio 3, let comedy fans move from Radio 4 to Radio 2. And we must ensure that TV viewers don't forget they've paid for radio as well and that all the riches of radio are also theirs for the taking.'

Whether or not the BBC has an unfair advantage over commercial broadcasters, their awareness that they have to 'sell' themselves is indica-tive of the changes in the radio industry since the mid-1990s. The point is that because of increased competition for a finite audience, *all* radio stations have to strive to brand themselves to encourage listener loyalty. At the BBC this is done through a team headed by the director of marketing and communications, but the strategies they use are the same ones used by all radio stations, which suggests that at root the non-commercial BBC is as much a business as any other radio station.

Station identity

The essential identity of a radio station is its output but this is much more than what music is played or the accent of the presenters. The station identity has to be reflected in the total sound of the station, or what Wilby and Conroy describe as 'a holistic concept of voice, music, language and topic which fit together in a coherent and inter-related way to create the station's own distinctive sound or "signature"' (1994: 40). This is generally achieved through written guidelines to presenters and producers about what sort of topics should be discussed, how much talk there should be between the music, and when regular features like news, traffic and travel information, weather reports, jingles and trailers should be run.

One of the attractions of radio is that it appears to be spontaneous, but the reality is that it is very carefully constructed with some tightly formatted stations literally scripting every second of output. Even on stations where there is more freedom for presenters to express themselves, this has to be done in a way that fits the station's identity. Too much talk on a music-based station can cause listeners who tune in for the music to go elsewhere. Similarly, discussing a topic that is not relevant to the audience on speech-based radio will cause listeners to retune.

'Some people will say "your link has to be 45 seconds long" but I don't do that,' explains the programme controller of Trent FM, Dick Stone.[6] 'What I say is talk for as long as you like but make sure every single second you speak is compelling and entertaining or shut up.'

The music

As previously mentioned, most radio stations in Britain are music based, and the style of music each station plays is a crucial aspect of the station's identity. Even stations more orientated to speech usually broadcast a few hours of music every week. In any event, the music played on most radio stations is not randomly selected by individual presenters but is governed by a music policy that has been developed to appeal to the station's target audience. At Radio 1, for example, the music it plays is seen as a key component of its audience's identity. 'Radio 1 does set out to give an identity about enjoying music and sharing a passion for music – travelling to live bands together . . . listening to the radio . . . logging on to the web site,' explains Radio 1 controller Andy Parfitt.[7] 'I believe Radio 1 carries out that role, and in fact I know it does because I listen to what the audience feeds back to us and there is that sense of community.'

But despite the popularity of music on radio, it is not the easy option it seems on the surface. In the first place it is expensive. Every piece of music played must be logged and details sent to the Performing Rights Society (PRS) who then charge royalties on behalf of the performers. Another problem is that even if a piece of music is popular, in that it is selling well, it may not be compatible with the overall sound of the station, so each piece of music has to be given careful consideration to ensure it will not make listeners reach for the dial or switch off. A third consideration is that the music played needs to reflect both the time of day and sequence in which it is played, so that the programme flows from one item to another rather than lurching around. Mellow love songs, for example, are generally regarded as being more appropriate to late-night shows, while more up-beat music is used in breakfast shows. For these reasons a carefully considered music policy is vital to every radio station.

Most music-based stations operate a playlist that is updated every week. The playlist determines what will be played, and how often it will be played. At small independent stations this is compiled by the programme controller often in collaboration with the head of music or other producers. Stations owned by a group, however, tend to have a group music policy so that their aural brand is consistent across all of their stations. In any event the selection of music is not down to personal taste but is a professional judgement that takes into account a variety of factors including the station's target audience, how appropriate a particular track is to certain times of the day, and often whether or not it has 'scored' well in audience research.

In line with many groups, GWR undertake extensive audience research about the music they play to come up with what they call 'today's better music mix'. As they state in their brand document, music 'is the central element of our product delivery – and a key reason for many listeners' choice.'

While this attitude may be expected on music-based systems, the importance of music is also recognised on speech-orientated stations to the extent that in 1998 the BBC developed a music policy for all of its 39 local stations that have a standard ratio of 70 per cent speech to 30 per cent music[8] targeting an audience of over-55-year-olds. BBC editor Kate Squire says the music policy is determined nationally but also allows 10 per cent of the playlist to be set locally. 'We play a core amount of music – about 1,200 tracks – that have all been very closely market researched for the 55-plus age group so that what you will tend to hear is classics from quite a wide range – Frank Sinatra, Shirley Bassey and lots of classic hits,' she explains. 'If you think about it people in their 50s and 60s now are the rock'n'roll generation so there's quite a lot of '60s, '70s and even contemporary music that's relevant.'

As with many aspects of radio, the way music is played, selected and logged has changed because of computerisation. The most widely used software package in commercial radio is the Selector system. This takes a pre-entered playlist and divides it by various categories like artist, title, tempo, mood and chart position and provides a running order. The running order takes into account how often the piece should be played over the day, which tracks should be played at a particular time of day, and makes sure the tracks flow together well.

The advantage of such a system to stations in a group is that it ensures a consistent sound effortlessly. It also gives every station an easy way to log what music has been used without filling out logging sheets and copyright returns. Moreover the system can either be adhered to rigidly or used in a more flexible way that allows presenters to select a 'special choice' every now and then. However, because the entire station's output is logged into the computer, it means that the details of any special choice – a listener's request for example – will automatically be shown, so presenters can see at a glance when the track was last played as well as how it is categorised and work out how appropriate it is for any particular slot.

Further developments in computers now mean that many stations store their music on hard disc that is accessed either by a fader system, touch-screen or keyboard. Adverts, jingles and station idents are also stored this way and can be played out automatically. While some see this as reducing the role of the presenter to that of a computer operator, the positive side of the system is that it frees presenters from endless logging and searching for the right track on CDs to do other things. This can range from setting up studio guests to answering calls from listeners or getting information updates to pass on in their programme.

Nonetheless there is a continuing debate on the effect systems like Selector are having on radio with some critics saying they contribute to a uniformity of output (see Barnard 2000: 132) but Dick Stone at Trent FM disagrees. 'I think Selector can take away some of the spontaneity of radio if it's in the wrong hands. I think in the right hands it can actually make it more effective,' he says. 'We hire people to transcend the format – they still do the format but they don't make it sound as if they're doing it – that's their skill. We don't hire them [presenters] to pick the music because they're not hired for their great music knowledge – they're hired to entertain and find something interesting to say.'

Another area of debate surrounds the use of fully automated programmes where the entire show is played out from a computer hard disk. This practice began in the 1990s but is becoming increasingly common especially on music-based stations for overnight and weekend slots. The advantage is that it cuts down labour costs but allows stations to provide local output that carries their aural brand. GWR FM in Bristol and Bath, for example, split their output to give Bath its own service which was fully automated, something the company say would not be possible any other way. However, the Radio Authority believes automation detracts from the localness of radio and wants to limit the amount commercial stations use. Advocates of the practice, however, say automated programmes provide a better service than the networked ones that many stations would be forced to use as an alternative because they can still have local references and content. 'It's a better programme done by a better jock who's not necessarily sitting in the studio because the technology we have now means it can sound as if they are,' says Dick Stone. 'A lot of Radio 1 and 2's programmes are automated – where's the debate about that? There isn't one because it doesn't affect the quality of what comes out of the speaker to the listener and that's what we should be focusing on – what the listener gets rather than how it's compiled. Automation is a tool just as having a tech op[9] is a tool – it's just a different way of doing things.'

Nonetheless, automated programming challenges the intimacy and 'liveness' of radio which are two of its most cherished attributes. The programmes may not sound any different from live radio, but the knowledge that what is being heard is not live could change the way it is received by listeners.

Jingles and ads

Music also features heavily in the jingles and commercials – either for products or other programmes – used on all radio stations and just like recorded music they have to blend with the overall sound of the station and reinforce its image. Jingles in particular play a vital branding function: they are an aural encapsulation of the station's image. As Wilby and Conroy observe, 'Jingles are regarded as vital in fixing the station's role and identity within the consciousness of the listening community' (1994: 55).

Jingles are used to punctuate a programme or link from one item to another, and they take various forms. A 'sting' can simply be a two-second burst of music used coming out of an ad break or as a pause between items. 'Lines' or 'station idents' that have music and give the station's name and frequency are used in a similar way. 'Sweepers' tend to be slightly longer but work in the same way, giving the station's name and frequency but also other information like the name of the show currently on-air, or naming various areas the station covers.

As well as punctuating the programme, jingles teach listeners the name and frequency of the station through constant repetition. As more stations become available it is vital that the frequency of the station is stated as often as possible so that it becomes embedded in the listener's consciousness. They also convey the style of the station instantly.

Although small stations may make some jingles in-house, their importance is such that most stations go to specialist companies who work with the station's marketing department to produce jingles that sum up the station's ethos. For example, Radio 1's jingles feature synthesised music and are up-beat, fast paced and direct in keeping with its 15–25-year-old target audience. The jingles on BBC local radio in stark contrast tend to be orchestrated and slower paced, often featuring various places in the station's transmission service area (TSA) to make each town feel part of the station.

'Trails' which are essentially adverts for other programmes on the station are usually done in-house because they are short lived by definition, but careful consideration is given to the style and music used in these as well. The idea of a trail is to tempt people to listen perhaps at a time they would not normally do so, and a poorly produced advert will have the opposite effect.

Commercial radio of course also broadcasts paid-for advertisements and both the content and scheduling of these can cause headaches for programme controllers. Dick Stone at Trent FM says that, although the quality of radio advertisements is improving, both technically and in their content, there are times when stations refuse to air some adverts either because they are not seen as 'tasteful' or because they are simply irritating. In these cases usually the client is persuaded to make changes to their advert.

And just as jingles have to be carefully scheduled to match the mood of programmes, there is a lot of consideration given to how adverts are run. Although the amount of advertising is limited by the Radio Authority to nine minutes in every hour, there are no rules about how this time should be divided up. As with all output, the primary concern of programme controllers is to play advertisements in the way that least annoys listeners so that they do not switch off. 'We tend to cluster our commercials in the daytime by having half an hour of music out of the news at the top of the hour and then the ad breaks in clusters in the up half hour,' explains Dick Stone. 'We then have half an hour of music and interrupt the music less. We interrupt it for longer, but there's research that shows that during the second commercial of any given break a certain percentage of people will tune out in any case so you might as well play three minutes of adverts because they're going to tune out anyway. Rather than playing a minute's worth often and stopping the music more often which irritates people, it's better to stop it less but for longer. That way people aren't irritated as much by the commercials and stay listening to the radio longer.'

The visual side of radio

The other kind of commercials that all radio uses are those that promote the station itself. Although an aural medium, radio requires a visual identity to make its presence known and establish its identity, especially at the launch of a new station when huge amounts of money are spent advertising on billboards, buses, television and in the press. Even established stations advertise themselves this way and encourage listeners to promote them with give-away car and window stickers bearing the station's logo and frequency.

The purpose of a logo is to give the station a visual identity. Most state the station's name and frequency in a way that conveys the character of the station. For example, talkSPORT conveys the station's character not

Local radio for Grimsby & Cleethorpes

LincsFMplc

Local Radio For The Wakefield District

Radio groups use the same style of logos for all their stations to identify them as belonging to the same group.

only by its name describing exactly what it is, but by having the first part of the name – 'talk' – in lower-case letters while 'sport' is in capital letters. This shows that although it is a talk station, the emphasis is firmly on sport, a fact that is further stressed through the logo being designed as a result board. The logo is also a way for local stations to be linked in groups. All local BBC stations, for example, have similar logos that give the brand BBC initials prominence, while the logos of stations in groups like Emap, GWR and Capital only differ in the station name and frequency.

Another way stations give themselves a visual identity is through outside broadcasts (OBs). These can range from full-scale roadshows where the station broadcasts live from shopping centres, factories, schools or special events, to the more low-key live links into programmes from a particular place. Most stations have a radio car that is essentially a mobile studio that can transmit from anywhere in the station's TSA. In the past these featured huge aerials that had to be erected with care to avoid overhead power lines, but since the late 1990s many are fitted with aerials the same as that of a standard car phone.

OBs are a way of reinforcing the station identity directly with the audience. 'We deliberately do a lot of outside broadcasts and we have the radio car out every day from 7 a.m. to 3 p.m. going to different places around the county providing snippets that can be fed into our programmes,' explains BBC Radio Nottingham editor Kate Squire. 'Our slogan is that we're at the heart of your community and we need to be visible out there. This is something that makes us different and it makes very good radio.'

In the past doing a radio show live from a particular location required a lot of pre-planning and expense with the hire of land lines costing thousands of pounds and truck-loads of technical equipment. More recently, however, OBs are done using ISDN lines that produce broadcast-quality sound for a few hundred pounds. Many locations like shopping centres, council buildings and football grounds already have ISDN points that can be plugged into using a shoebox-sized pack that is a codec – that converts analogue audio into digital form for transfer over ISDN – and mixer combined. Some stations even have ISDN lines installed at the homes of key personnel so that they can broadcast from there in the event of an emergency that prevents them from using their studios.

Concerts, campaigns and competitions

Another way for radio stations to connect with their audience and reinforce their brand identity is through promoting or sponsoring events. Music radio stations at both a national and local level often sponsor concerts that reflect the style of music they play. The Proms, for example, are the highlight of BBC Radio 3's year and a prestigious way for the station to emphasise its commitment to classical music. Similarly Capital Radio in London holds an annual 'Party in the Park' featuring a wide range of pop acts designed to appeal to its audience. These events not only provide stations with live material that can be used in programmes, they also give them a chance to reach potential new listeners through the publicity such events attract from other media.

Charity events and campaigns on radio also help stations to keep a high profile. Many BBC local stations hold an annual radio auction to raise money for a local cause, and BBC Radio 1's campaigns to inform their audience about social issues like drug and alcohol abuse, sexual health and student finances are justifiably renowned.

However, campaigns need to be carefully thought through to make sure the cause is one that is relevant to the audience and done in a style that is compatible with the station's image. Lincs FM, for example, had a campaign to encourage people to donate blood where donors who said they had heard about it on the radio were given a special 'beany blood drop'. The campaign resulted in an increase in donors in the area and reinforced

the station's image as being family orientated, but at no time was it allowed
to dominate programme output. 'Our listeners are not necessarily people
who would want to listen to "worthy" radio,' explains the group director
of programmes Jane Hill. 'But if in the course of their normal working
day and while listening to some good music they hear the presenter say
"ever thought about giving some blood?" – that actually works.'

Judging from the profusion of high-profile competitions run by almost
every radio station in the country, however, it seems that on-air contests
are the most popular way to try to hook listeners into the station. Virgin
Radio created the first 'radio millionaire' by giving away a million pounds
on Christmas Eve 1999 as the climax of a quiz held over the preceding
months, while Radio 1 often has competitions where the prizes are tickets
to a pop concert or a special event like a film premiere.

Competitions are a way for the station to interact with the audience
and underpin the values of their brand. Stations often use them to try to
boost listening figures at particular times of the day and where the prize
is unusual or spectacular to give them publicity elsewhere.

In some cases, however, the publicity is not always good, as BRMB
in Birmingham discovered when they organised a competition called 'Love
on the Airwaves' that culminated in the 'winners' getting married. The
contest began in November 1998 and featured psychologists, counsellors
and astrologers analysing applications from 100 men and 110 women to
find the most compatible couple, who met each other for the first time at
their wedding ceremony in January 1999. As well as footing the bill for
the wedding, including gold rings inscribed with the station name and call
sign, BRMB also paid for a luxury honeymoon in the Caribbean and gave
the couple a flat in central Birmingham and the use of a car for a year.
Predictably the marriage failed after just 12 weeks.

From the moment the competition was announced BRMB came under
attack from Church leaders and marriage guidance associations for trivi-
alising marriage, and further publicity was given through a television documentary made about the couple, and a *News of the World* exclusive with
them. The project reportedly cost the station £50,000 and although it generated months of high-profile publicity, this has to be balanced against the
fact that many people felt the competition was tasteless and that the station
exploited the couple for its own ends.

As we have seen, branding a radio station is important to give a visual
identity to an invisible service. But the most important part of any station
is the people whose voices are heard by the audience – the presenters,

newsreaders and reporters. Presenters in particular can inspire fierce loyalty in listeners and often take their audience with them when they change stations (Hargrave 2000: 15). They are literally the voice of the station and, according to Chris Hughes of the GWR group, it is the presenter that makes the difference to a station. 'You can give one presenter the same records, the same commercials, the same news bulletins, the same links and put them on for an hour and they'll have different ratings to somebody doing exactly the same thing. There's some indescribable magic quality in those people,' he says.

The following chapter looks at the voice of the station through an examination of the role of presenters on both talk- and music-based stations. It ends with transcripts from three different stations and a brief analysis of their content.

Notes

1   Quoted in the GWR Brand document 2000.
2   All quotations from Phil Dixon from author interview, October 2000.
3   All quotations from Kate Squire from author interview, October 2000.
4   All quotations from Jane Hill from author interview, October 2000.
5   Available at www.bbc.co.uk/info/editorial/prodgl/index.shtml.
6   All quotations from Dick Stone from author interview, November 2000.
7   All quotations from Andy Parfitt from author interview, July 2001.
8   The exception to this ratio is the London-based BBC station that targets a slightly different audience to other BBC local stations.
9   A 'tech op' is a technical operator who operates a studio desk to drive the programme as it goes out.

4 The voice of the station

....

Whether music or speech-based, radio relies on the human voice to connect with the audience. As Andrew Crisell points out, 'radio is a "live" predominantly *personal* medium and un-relieved music with no visible human origination is dauntingly *im*personal' (1986: 65). In other words it is the voices of presenters and newsreaders that we most respond to on the radio. They are the personification of radio providing a personality with which we identify and connect.

'A good presenter is a person who's in touch with and sympathetic to and part of the lifestyle of the person they are broadcasting to,' explains Chris Hughes of the GWR group. 'They've got to be seen by the listeners in several different ways all at the same time. Young girls have got to fancy them, older women want to mother them, blokes want to have a drink with them. They've got to be hardworking, they've got to be excited by the medium, and they've got to be in touch with the people they're broadcasting to.'

From that description it is clear that the job of a radio presenter is much more than simply talking between the music. What they say and the way they say it are important in reinforcing the station brand and establishing a relationship with the audience. There are various presentation styles and techniques but at root the role of the presenter is to be the station's representative to the audience – the embodiment of the brand – and to represent the audience on-air – to be 'just like us'. Obviously, different styles of radio require different skills from presenters, and this chapter examines the skills used by presenters on various stations.

Presenter functions

The primary function of a presenter is to create a bond with the listener that will keep them tuning in to the station. As Dick Stone at Trent FM puts it, 'Teaching listeners the name of the station is the number-one job of a presenter. Their next job is to get anyone who's listening now to listen for the next five minutes.'[1]

This is true of speech radio as well as music radio, and although there are devices like jingles and trails for what is coming up later, the basic tool a presenter has is her or his voice. As Wilby and Conroy explain,

> The voice may inform, announce, comment, ask questions, pass on gossip or attempt to persuade – whatever mode of address it adopts, it constitutes the key to the radio experience. Records and jingles contribute to an overall style of a station's output but the voice actually says something that listeners should latch on to, remember and talk about.
>
> (1994: 128)

Thankfully the days when music station DJs adopted a mid-Atlantic accent and speech stations were dominated by Home County accents are long gone. British radio now has a rich mix of regional accents on both local and national radio and the advice given by Elwyn Evans, a former head of the BBC's Radio Training Unit, is still pertinent. 'Don't put on any sort of act; your ordinary way of speaking is perfectly all right: if it weren't, you wouldn't have been asked to broadcast' (1977: 20).

That said, sounding 'natural' while addressing a microphone in a studio is more difficult than it first seems and many stations spend a lot of time, especially with new staff, on voice training done either by senior staff or specialists brought in for training sessions.

Voices and scripts

The point of voice training is not to change the accent of presenters but to help them use the full range of their voices so that what they say is clear and delivered in a relaxed, confident manner. Most voice trainers spend a lot of time teaching new broadcasters how to breathe deeply, using their diaphragm. This technique is useful for two reasons. The first is that deep breathing prevents any nervousness coming out in the voice, and the second is that it usually has the effect of lowering the voice to make it sound more resonant and authoritative. In order to breathe deeply more easily, many trainers recommend that new broadcasters stand in front of the microphone or at the very least sit up straight. Sitting hunched over the microphone encourages shallow breathing that often makes the voice sound squeaky.

Another tip from voice trainers is to do a few mouth exercises before going on air to loosen the muscles and help prevent tripping over words. According to veteran BBC presenter Sue MacGregor, presenters should also avoid drinking fruit juice before broadcasting, as it tends to make your mouth water. If you feel your mouth drying, stick to water.

Voice training can be very useful in helping broadcasters to realise the full potential of their voices but it is not a substitute for practice and an important part of practising should be listening back to yourself. Only by listening to the way you sound to other people can you pick out when your voice has slipped into a monotone or when you sound inappropriately enthusiastic.

But as Elwyn Evans stresses, the most important aspect of broadcasting is to maintain the right attitude. 'The listener needs to feel that he is being spoken to personally. This can only happen if the broadcaster feels that he himself is talking personally, to a particular individual' (1977: 20). While this may be easier to achieve when presenters are not reading from a script, as on most music stations, it is also vital in speech-based programmes.

So why bother with scripts at all? Surely it would sound better if the presenter simply spoke about topics aided by a few key notes? In theory this might be better and some experienced broadcasters do just that, but in practice there are good reasons for scripting most speech-based programmes.

First of all a script takes some of the pressure off presenters doing live broadcasts. Presenters have enough pressure during a live programme – driving the desk, lining up inserts, dealing with studio guests or interviews down the line, watching the clock – without also having to speak coherently on a variety of topics off the top of their head. A script provides them with the reassurance that they know what they are going to say next so that they can concentrate on *how* they say it. Many broadcasters even write out their introduction to programmes: 'Good morning and welcome to the programme – I'm John Smith and today we're going to . . .' This is not because they do not know what their name is or what is in the programme, but because having it written down means they do not have to remember it, so they can concentrate on their delivery of the words and make sure the words flow well.

Scripts also ensure that an item is covered fully, in a logical manner and to a set time. Just try doing a film review for exactly two minutes off the top of your head – the chances are you will either run out of time before you have covered all the points you want to make, or you will deal with the film in a minute and a half and have to waffle for 30 seconds! A script ensures the duration is accurate and that the review unfolds in an interesting way.

As will be dealt with in more detail below, writing for listeners is quite different from writing for readers. The tone of a broadcast script should be conversational and relaxed with verbs abbreviated to help the piece flow. Sentences should be simple and short with the minimum amount of punctuation. Indeed some broadcasters prefer to write scripts as a series of phrases, arguing that very little conversation is in proper sentences and linked phrases give scripts more 'life'. In any event the language used should be colloquial rather than formal with facts spread evenly through the script. Most important of all, the presenter must be interested in what she or he is saying: without that there is no hope of engaging with listeners.

Take, for example, the following link into a live report on BBC 5 Live that deals with the fuel protests in November 2000:

> Let's go back to the fuel protestors driving south from Newcastle – what they were calling . . . for a while . . . the Jarrow Crusade Mark Two – we've nicknamed it Convoy GB . . . we updated last about an hour ago with Doug Morris . . . now it's Mark James for 5 Live . . . Mark, are there more 5 Live reporters there than truck drivers?

The tone of this link is conversational with linked phrases rather than a formal sentence structure, and inclusive with the use of 'let's go back to' that involves the listener immediately rather than the more formal 'we now return to'. The reference to a previous report tells listeners who may not have heard it that this is an ongoing event without reiterating what was previously said, and although the reporter is fully introduced, using his first name only for the initial question makes the piece sound more like a conversation than a formal interview. Moreover, the question itself tells listeners that the convoy is not as big as had been expected without actually spelling it out. This not only avoids information broadcast earlier being repeated, which would be boring for those who have already heard the earlier reports, it also allows listeners to conjure up a picture of the media trailing their way down the M1 causing more trouble than the few protestors.

Writing for radio[2]

As the above example shows, the key principle of writing for radio is that it is not being written to be read, but to be *spoken* – often by someone other than the writer – and *heard*. Putting this into practice is more difficult than it seems because writing as we speak involves abandoning many of the 'rules' of writing that have been taught to us from an early age. We need to concentrate on how the piece *sounds* rather than how it looks written on the page.

As Robert McLeish points out, 'writing words on paper is a very crude form of storage' (1988: 48), because while written words convey information they do not convey the full meaning. What should be emphasised? Where do the pauses come? What speed should it be read at? What is the tone of the piece? For example the simple statement, 'I am going out now' can convey different meanings depending on the way it is said. '*I* am going out now'; 'I *am* going out now'; 'I'm going *out* now'; 'I'm going out *now*' – and so on. If you read these statements aloud you will see how each conveys a subtly different meaning.

As previously mentioned, one of the strengths of radio is that it speaks to individuals, and the way it does this is by *talking* to them, not *reading* to them. This means that whatever is said on the radio – whether it is a link in a magazine programme, a film review, or even a voice piece in the news – needs to sound as if it is coming from the mind of the speaker – almost like part of a conversation – rather than something that is being read. While underlining certain words and presentation skills can aid this process, the way a script is written is also important, as we will see below.

It is often said that radio writing is conversational. But a conversation involves more than one person, so a good starting place before beginning writing is to visualise the person you are talking to – a typical member of the station's audience. Although the audience may be older or younger than you, essentially they will be on the same level as you, so there is no need to use language to try to impress them, or to take a simplistic approach that might come across as patronising. In writing a film review for a BBC local radio audience, for example, think about how you would tell your grandmother about the film. In reviewing a pop concert for an ILR station, think about how you would tell your friend about the band.

Visualising who you are speaking to also helps to remind you that although what you are saying is being heard by a mass audience, each member of the audience receives your words as an individual. Logically we all know that what is said on the radio is being heard by many people, but the words have much more impact if each person feels they are being spoken to directly. One way to connect with the individual is to include them in what you are saying. This can be done by referring to 'us' and 'we', rather than the much more impersonal 'listeners' or 'the audience'. For example, you might start a film review by saying, 'Most of us enjoy a night out at the pictures' or a pop concert review with the words, 'We all know bands that look great on video but let themselves down in live performances'. This immediately includes listeners in what is being said.

Once you know who you are talking to, the next thing is to work out what you are going to say. Although writing for radio is conversational, unlike a conversation there is no chance for the person listening to you to ask you to repeat what you have just said, or ask questions about something they do not quite understand. For those reasons it is important that your script is logical and progresses at an even pace. Work out what points you want to make, then see how they all connect together in a way that makes sense.

Your first sentence is vitally important. This is the 'hook' that will grab the attention of the listener. There is no need to ease into the topic gradually. The first sentence needs to be intriguing but relevant, and be backed by a second sentence that explains what you are talking about. Avoid packing too much information into one sentence: a rough rule of thumb is to have one idea per sentence, which logically links into the next sentence. Try to remember that you are not just imparting information – you are telling a story and you need to keep the audience with you every step of the way.

The best scripts allow listeners to visualise what you're describing. Too many facts too close together will cause confusion rather than pictures, so space the information out evenly and provide concrete images that explain facts. For example, instead of giving the physical dimensions of a field, describe it as being the size of a football pitch; if you are talking about a tall building, relate it to a ten-storey block of flats.

You also need to be careful with the use of abbreviations and acronyms. Only a few are well enough known to be understood straight away by most people. So, while it is fine to refer to the BBC or Aids without spelling them out, others should be explained the first time you use them. For example, the first time you refer to the National Union of Journalists you could say 'the journalists' union, the NUJ . . .' so that the next time you use 'NUJ' everyone knows that it is a trade union for journalists. Similarly, the first time you refer to someone in your script, you need to explain who they are or give their position. Never assume that just because *you* know who they are, everyone else will. For example you might say, 'film director Ridley Scott' or 'Tim Fullbright, the leader of the City Council'.

The language you use in writing for radio can also help it to sound more conversational. Use everyday language and avoid literary or academic words. Keep the language simple and direct and make sure you translate jargon. For example, in describing a new sports complex it is better to say 'the complex is built on what used to be a children's play area' rather than 'the complex was erected on a former recreation area for children'.

Your language needs to be colloquial – which is not the same as sloppy or slang. What it means is that it needs to sound like ordinary conversation. This means abbreviating verbs where you can, so that 'it is' becomes 'it's', 'would not' becomes 'wouldn't'. Should you want special emphasis you can revert to the full form: 'Tony Blair says he will not back down' rather than 'Tony Blair says he won't back down'.

Speech also tends to use shorter sentences that have a simple construction. Short sentences are both easier to understand and easier to read. For example, 'The dress, previously owned by the pop star Madonna, and designed by Stella McCartney, was destroyed in the fire' is more difficult to take in than 'The dress destroyed in the fire used to belong to pop star Madonna. It was designed by Stella McCartney', and it also *sounds* more natural.

But the best way to make sure you are writing as you talk is to speak the story out loud and write down what you say. You can always tidy your script up to make it more polished after you have finished it, and this is more effective than writing it and then making changes to make it sound conversational. Saying your script out loud also helps you to avoid tongue twisters or words that you might find awkward to pronounce. It is not enough to read it to yourself: scripts read in your head always sound perfect.

Scripts should be set out as clearly as possible. Use a large typeface, double spaced, so that any small alterations can be made without rendering the piece unreadable. Sentences should not run over to the next page. Indeed, ideally paragraphs should not be split between pages given that there is a slightly longer pause between paragraphs than sentences.

A lot of what you write will be read by someone else, so to help them get the exact sense of what is written you need to use clear punctuation. Do not write scripts in upper case only. This makes it more difficult for the reader to see when a new sentence begins, or when a 'proper' name is used. As a general rule, less punctuation is better. It is easier to interpret a dash than a semicolon, and a sentence punctuated by a series of commas is usually better broken down into several shorter sentences.

Dealing with numbers in scripts can be tricky and the safest way is to write them out in full – especially those over six figures. It is very easy for the eye to miss a zero, so rather than 'more than £2,000,000' write 'more than two million pounds'. This will also help you to get a more accurate duration for your piece using the standard calculation of three words per second. When using numbers in the first line of a piece it is also best to simplify them and give the detail further down the script. For example say, 'nearly half the population go abroad on holiday', rather than, 'forty-eight point seven per cent of the population go abroad on holiday'.

If the piece you are writing is complex do not be afraid to repeat ideas but find a different way of expressing them. For example, you can use phrases like 'what's meant by that is . . .' or 'in practice that means . . .' to indicate a fuller explanation of a point.

Finally, a script should have a definite ending rather than just stop. Just as the first sentence of a script needs to catch the listener's interest, the last sentence should give them food for thought. This can be in the form of a provocative question, or a statement that concisely sums up the item. Ideally the end of a piece should refer back to the beginning and act as a reminder of your arguments or views. What should be avoided are clichéd phrases like 'only time will tell' that leave the piece hanging in the air. The beginning and end of a script are the most important parts of it and also the parts most people will remember.

The 'good' presenter

There are probably as many definitions of a 'good' presenter as there are radio stations. Each station wants presenters that reinforce its brand values:

in other words, the personality they project should connect with that of the station's target audience. As Andy Parfitt, the controller of Radio 1 explains, at a station like his it is vital to have a knowledge of and interest in music without being patronising. 'I think the key is about being authentic – we don't really have people on who're pretending to be personalities,' he says.[3] 'We go for people who know the music and have an empathy for the music – who understand the audience and can entertain but by being real and being able to talk to the audience in a normal, ordinary way. Being at one with the audience and delivering the music are the key credentials.'

On other stations, other skills are also valued. Most local radio stations, for example, like to stress their 'localness' not only through the accents of their presenters but also through their knowledge of the area. For BBC local radio, which targets an older audience, local knowledge is vital in helping to establish a link between the station and the audience. 'What makes a good presenter is someone who is rooted in the local commu-nity, who knows the place, who knows the place names, who knows the history,' says BBC editor Kate Squire.[4]

And while local knowledge is also important on commercial stations, Dick Stone of Trent FM says presenters also have to have the ability to transcend the format that music-based stations run to. 'No one wakes up in the morning and thinks "I think I'll have a bit of adult contemporary music today" – that doesn't happen,' he says. 'People think "I like the music on that station" or "that person entertains me" or "that person relates to the way I live my life". So a good presenter is someone who takes the format of the station – which is the technical way you take an ad break or when you play ids – and turns it into something that does more than that – something that communicates to somebody.'

However, there is more to a presenter's job than what they say on-air and a lot of work goes into preparing programmes. Usually the programme controller, producer or editor holds regular 'post-mortem' sessions that examine the programmes to see what items worked well and what went wrong. Because presenters drive their own programmes, controlling the computer system and sound desk from the studio on their own, this can cover technical faults as well as the content.

The preparation for a radio programme is vital and, as the profiles that follow show, it can dominate the lives of presenters. Whether on a speech-based or music-based station, presenters need to know what is happening in the world so they spend a lot of time reading newspapers and listening and watching news bulletins. Most radio studios have a television in them so that even while on-air presenters can keep up to date by monitoring Ceefax and Teletext. Presenters are also the public face of the station so they are expected to take part in station promotions, visiting schools and colleges, opening fetes, and giving talks to various social groups. On top of this, smaller stations also expect their presenters to do work for other programmes when they are not on-air. This can range from scheduling music to preparing community news or making a package (see Glossary and pp. 109–112).

But however skilled a presenter is, it is the station and not the presenter who is the 'star'. As Jane Hill of the Lincs FM group points out, 'Everybody knows Chris Tarrant but I'm not sure how many people know which radio station he works for – he's bigger than the station and that can be quite dangerous. We wouldn't be able to keep someone who was getting offers from other places so for a smaller station you have to make the station the star and we have to have presenters who understand that.'[5]

Being a presenter is not the straightforward job it appears to most people. It requires a wide range of skills and as the profiles that follow show, dedication to the job. What also comes across from the profiles is that an awareness of the audience and an understanding of their needs and expectations are vital for presenters to do their job effectively.

Profile | Jane Franchi, BBC Scotland
Presenting live news

BBC Radio Scotland is a national regional station that is predominantly a speech-based station targeting 35–54-year-olds but it also has music programmes for younger listeners. Its flagship programme is *Good Morning Scotland* that broadcasts from 6–8.45 a.m. on weekday mornings to the whole of Scotland from studios in Glasgow. The programme covers international and national news from a Scottish perspective and is similar in style to Radio 4's *Today* programme, with a team of regular presenters, supplemented from time to time by other journalists like Jane Franchi.[6]

Like many BBC journalists, Jane is bi-media and alternates between radio and television work, and she admits that presenting *Good Morning Scotland* is a high-pressure job. 'We're on air for nearly

Jane Franchi of BBC Radio Scotland.

Photo courtesy of BBC Radio Scotland.

three hours at a time when news across the world and here too is changing the whole time,' she says.[7] This means there is constant pressure to keep up to date with stories across the world, especially as the style of the programme is for the two presenters – usually a man and a woman – to do live interviews: it is not enough just to know what is happening now; you also have to know the background to stories.

Jane presents four mornings a week and her day begins at 3 a.m. 'Eventually your body-clock gets used to it,' she says. 'Day three is the absolute killer – that's the one when your legs are like lead, your eyes ache, your brain's a blancmange and you feel that you're never going to get your head around anything.'

Over several cups of tea Jane checks Ceefax to see if anything has changed overnight, reading every story to make sure she is as well briefed as possible. By the time she gets to the studios at about 4.30 a.m. she has a good idea of what is happening in the world and can start her 'real' work.

'Occasionally between half past four and six when we go on air – given the time of day it is all over the world – it may be that we have to pre-record an interview that then goes out "as-live",' she explains. 'I go through all the material in the programme and read the briefing notes and read as much as I can of the newspapers.' Reading the papers is important not only because there are three slots in the programme that review them, but also because they can sometimes suggest questions that can be used in later interviews.

Although it is the presenters' responsibility to keep abreast of news, they are helped by a team of journalists who provide background notes for stories that are known about the night before. 'There's a very good team on *Good Morning Scotland* and I'm constantly boggled by the amount of information they have,' Jane says. 'Normally we get a briefing note for a story that states what the aim of the interview is and what they want to learn from it. Things change over the course of the programme so a list of questions is pointless. Also if you have a list of questions you tend not to listen to the answer – you just go to the next question and that's not a way I or any of my colleagues work. You must listen to the answers because often there's something that can be picked up from that.'

Jane describes the style of interviewing on the programme as challenging but not confrontational and admits that an important part of her job is sensing how the interview should be pitched. 'If you're interviewing somebody who's not used to it, then part of my job is to put that person at ease,' she explains. 'This can be quite difficult if you don't have eye-contact with them and frequently you don't – they're often somewhere else – in many cases in a self-operating studio staring at a white wall – and you've got no time to talk to them beforehand. You introduce them and that's you on-air with them and you pick up very quickly whether they're at ease or not.'

However, Jane believes that politicians are fair game because they are trained to deal with the media often to the point of avoiding answering questions. This gives presenters a different kind of problem. 'There's a very fine line between you trying to bring the person back to the point you feel the listener wants to be answered, without appearing rude and aggressive, and the listeners not liking the interviewer because they're perceived to be bullying,' she says. 'At the same time you've got to recognise that there are people who are extraordinarily skilled at making it sound as if they're answering questions when they're not, and if you're a news and current affairs programme these are things you've got to challenge.'

Another consideration that the programme has to deal with is the fact that it covers the whole of Scotland and there is a need to get a good geographical spread of stories every morning. This is helped by BBC local stations in Scotland, who feed stories and information to Glasgow, as well as the presenters' knowledge of the country. 'I live in Aberdeen and spent 15 years working for the BBC there so I have a north-east perspective on things and there is an acute consciousness among everybody on the programme that we cover the whole country,' Jane explains. 'But you can't manufacture items and God forbid that we say, 'Oh it's from Shetland so we must carry it' – we don't do that. What we do is if, for example, the Scottish Parliament makes an announcement and it affects somebody in Cambuslang differently from somebody in Shetland we try to reflect that.'

From the moment the programme goes on air the presenters are under pressure not only to keep it flowing but also to update stories. 'There's the occasional dive out of the studio – one at seven o'clock and one at eight o'clock when it's a ten-minute news bulletin – but frequently during that eight minutes or whatever you have you have to do another pre-recorded interview with somebody who simply cannot do it live. Which brings me to the last thing that you've got to have and that's an incredibly strong bladder – at seven and eight it can be a loo break and a quick swallow of coffee but if you're involved in a pre-record you're gassed.'

After the programme editors, producers, journalists and presenters all meet to go over its good and bad points. Then Jane aims to be home for 10.30 a.m. to unwind before sleeping between 2 p.m. and 4.30 p.m. But the job does not end then. Every night at 7.30 p.m. the programme's producer puts in a conference call to the presenters and the morning producer to discuss the next day's schedule and go over any particular items that are already known about. Then it is a constant diet of news from radio and television until the next sleep time. 'I never miss a single radio or television news in case something happens or in case they can give me a different slant on a story which is inevitably going to crop up,' Jane says. 'When the BBC news was on at nine I was in bed by ten – now I feel obliged to watch the head-lines at least. If nothing's changed dramatically I'll go to bed but if something's developed I'll stay and watch it, but if I'm not in bed by 10.20 I'll certainly feel it the next day.'

The demands of the job are immense but Jane thinks presenting is less emotionally demanding than the investigative work journalists do for documentaries. 'When you've finished your shift you can at least go home and somehow you don't take the burden of it with you the way you do when you're doing a documentary,' she says. 'It seems my whole life is dominated by the job but I love it and I never wanted to do anything else.'

Profile | Jo and Twiggy, Trent FM
Breakfast chat

To the outsider it may seem that presenting a music-based show requires a lot less preparation than doing a news programme, but for Jo and Twiggy who host the breakfast show on Nottingham's Trent FM the demands of the job are different but just as all-consuming.

'You do the prep for the show the day and night before,' explains 29-year-old Joanna Russell. 'We don't have a script but we know what topics we're going to talk about and we often record interviews the day before because most people don't want to get up at six in the

Jo (Joanne Russell) and Twiggy (Andy Twigge), breakfast show presenters on
Trent FM.

Photo courtesy of Trent FM, Nottingham.

morning. The thing about doing a breakfast show is that by the time
we go to bed and get up the next morning the whole show could be
completely different depending on what's happened overnight.'

Jo and her co-presenter Twiggy – whose full name is Andy Twigge
– teamed up for the breakfast show on Trent in 1998 and are used to
the early-morning start that requires them to be in the studios by 5 a.m.
at the latest to go on-air from 6–9 a.m. 'I very rarely have to set my
alarm now,' says Twiggy. 'I just automatically wake up.' They describe their show as having a 'Morecambe and Wise feel' to it with a
lot of banter between themselves, other members of the production
team, and the audience. 'We're like a family really,' says Twiggy
who is known for his quick-witted wisecracks.

The first job on arrival at the studio is to go through the morning
newspapers to be up to date with news stories and also to find amusing
stories that can be discussed on-air. Some features of the programme
like competitions and traffic news are scheduled for particular times,
but the duo try to make the show sound as spontaneous as possible.
'What we aim to do is talk about what people will be talking about
for the rest of the day,' explains Jo. This can range from news topics
to soap-opera gossip, but Twiggy acknowledges that they tend to

concentrate on the lighter side of the news. 'If there was something major going on in the news you wouldn't come to us – you'd probably go to Radio 4,' he says. 'We'll do snippets of important news stories but if you wanted to really know what's going on you wouldn't come to us.' The exception, says Jo, is when a big news story happens locally. 'If there was a big train crash in Nottingham we would suspend all programming and just talk about that – it's how it affects people in Nottingham and Mansfield and it's as simple as that,' she says.

Originally from York, Jo started her radio career in hospital broadcasting before getting the overnight shift at Minster FM in York. 'I used to get to the studios at midnight, do my show, do some prep for the next day's show and then do a full day's work at General Accident [the insurance company where Jo had a day job before she became a full-time broadcaster] before going to sleep from about half past five to eleven at night,' she says. 'It was like having two full-time jobs but I didn't want to leave the insurance company because I didn't have a contract. Even with a contract it's a dodgy business, but without one . . .'

Twiggy's entry to radio was less conventional. He just drifted into it, he says, after a series of jobs including being a milkman, a lorry driver and selling sandwiches on the beach in St Tropez. His radio career began on Ram FM in Derby where he was part of a zoo format (where the main presenter is joined on-air by other 'characters' who all contribute spontaneously to the show) on the breakfast show and did outside broadcasts. From there he moved on to working with Jo, initially in Derby and then in Nottingham. 'The best thing about the job is being on-air but the next best thing is being on-air with someone you really get on with,' he says. 'It's far better to work as a team because it's more fun doing it with other people.'

An important part of the preparation for the show involves watching soap operas and other popular shows on television. 'It's funny because when you watch TV you watch it in a completely different way,' says Jo. 'You don't sit down and relax and watch a soap opera, you sit down and watch it and think "how can I talk about this on-air tomorrow?"'

The programme has input from the producer and the programme controller and there is an hour-long meeting after every show to discuss it and plan future features or outside broadcasts. Although the pair have a lot of freedom about what they talk about, they tend to avoid certain topics (such as politics) or stories involving sex (such as the Gary Glitter case in 1999).

Unusually, the desk is controlled by Jo. 'I think it's really important to know how to drive the desk,' she says. 'It means that if you're in a crew you've always got the option to go off and do something by yourself. There are a lot of females that don't drive the desk and have never had to and they're going to be really stuffed if it all goes wrong.'

Another important part of the job is promotion work visiting schools, summer fetes and Christmas fairs. Both presenters take this seriously; it's a way for people who don't listen to them to find out about them and perhaps give the show a try. Both work hard to promote the station and like to feel that they are approachable. 'Someone said to Twiggy the other day, "I really like you because you're one of us", and I hope that is the case,' says Jo. 'I would hate to think that people felt they couldn't approach us.'

But being in the public eye means that even when they are out socially they can be approached by listeners, and not all of them are fans. 'The hardest part for me is when people walk up to me and say "you're crap" – it's just rude and what right have they got to say that?' says Twiggy. 'I mean our product is free – we don't charge them to listen – but people think they can do that to us.'

Despite this, both presenters enjoy their work to the extent that for six weeks in 1999 Twiggy presented his part of the show from his home via an ISDN line while he was recovering from a leg operation. 'I love radio and I always knew this was what I wanted to do,' says Jo. 'The best bit of the job without a doubt is being on-air from six till nine – coming in and knowing that you can gas to your mates – and you're getting paid for it!'

Profile | Alan Clifford, BBC Radio Nottingham

From pirate to presenter

Like most local BBC stations, Radio Nottingham targets an audience of 55-year-olds with a mix of 70 per cent speech to 30 per cent music, which means their presenters have to be able to switch from dealing

Presenter Alan Clifford outside BBC East Midlands studios.

Photo courtesy of BBC Radio Nottingham.

with serious news to a lighter, chattier style interspersed with music, depending which programme they are working on and what time it is going out.

Alan Clifford who presents the station's drive-time show from 5–7 p.m. says at times this can be difficult. 'Sometimes you might have to give a politician or a councillor or a company representative a hard time, and then literally in the next interview you have to be very sympathetic with somebody who's just lost a relative in tragic circumstances and then after six o'clock it's more like being a disc jockey and chatting amiably about life,' he says.

'Trying to marry hard-hitting current affairs with Sid and Doris having their cup of tea at home is quite difficult. You might approach an interview in a certain way and then afterwards people would say you needed to be more forthright or a bit more pointed and I would say "well, I'm not sure that's what our audience wants to hear". You have to marry not only what you think your audience wants but what you know your boss wants.'

All this is a far cry from Alan's first broadcasting experiences on various pirate radio stations that he joined after being inspired by the alternative music played on Radio Caroline. 'The thought of sitting in the North Sea on a boat playing obscure album tracks really appealed to me,' he explains. So while studying for a degree in electronics and computer science he spent a lot of time doing illegal broadcasting. 'It was a very low-powered FM transmitter and probably no one really listened but it was a kind of social group and it was fun to do and all the time I was learning production techniques,' he says.

On graduation he joined an unlicensed station based in Ireland with 'an audience of four men and a sheep' before joining the BBC as an audio assistant based at Pebble Mill. Over the next few years Alan cajoled and nagged his way to doing various bits of broadcasting on local stations in Birmingham, Leicester and Nottingham. 'Eventually I got to work on the mid-morning show on Radio Nottingham going out in the radio car doing two packages a day, live interviews, whatever you could really,' he explains. 'Then came the week when more than one of the regular presenters was off and I was thrown in to do the lunch-time show.'

Since then Alan has presented most of the Radio Nottingham programmes at one time or another and he admits the breakfast programme that he did for two years carries the most pressure. 'The pressure's not only when you're broadcasting – when you're finished, you know, you've got to go to a meeting and somebody's going to pick holes in what you've done,' he says. 'At breakfast you're more likely to get breaking stories and there can be a lot of pressure when you're interviewing somebody live and you've got somebody telling you in your headphones what question to ask when you've got perfectly good questions of your own. Not only is that a distraction but you've got to make a decision – is that question better than the one I was going to ask, does it fit better with the answer that's been given? – well, I don't know because I've not heard it because some-body's been talking in my headphones!'

Like most broadcasters, Alan agrees that interviews with politi-cians need to be carefully handled. 'With politicians you have to get them off their guard and when you're working to a fixed agenda that can be very difficult because there are questions you feel you have to ask,' he explains. He recalls an interview with the Prime Minister Tony Blair in November 2000 when Britain was coping with wide-spread floods, and the Chancellor's pre-budget speech had announced changes for pensioners but had not delivered the cuts to fuel duty that protestors were demanding. 'That was a very unsatisfying interview for me because it was agreed that those were the areas that I was going to talk about but it meant that he just trotted out the same answers,' says Alan. 'It would've been better with hindsight to have said, "with all these problems of floods, pensions and fuel are you looking forward to maybe not being Prime Minister after the next election?" That would've been a much better question because he would have had to have thought of an answer – with the benefit of hindsight you can always think of better questions.'

Alan agrees that preparation is the key to good broadcasting but on small stations the luxury of focusing on just one programme does not exist. Presenters have to contribute material for other programmes, do promotional work for the station, as well as various administra-tive duties. 'You get pulled in a lot of different directions and some-times you can end up relying on other people writing questions about a topic you have no prior knowledge of,' he says.

But despite the pressures Alan enjoys his work and over the years he has built up an understanding of the audience and a knowledge of the area he broadcasts to that is vital in local radio. 'Sometimes people can work to a news agenda and the locality aspect is lost – you have to know your area,' he says. 'I would like to see as part of induction to the station people given a day and a fleet car to visit a series of places with a few questions to answer about them and for them to come back with four story ideas. That would force people at least to get a basic idea of the geography.'

For him the best programmes are those that actually make a difference to the lives of the people listening, as happened in November 2000 when his programme was extended for four hours every night for a week to keep people up to date with flood news. 'One night I had to give the Environment Agency a hard time about their flood-line number which was next to useless because people couldn't get through and the call after that was somebody on a mobile watching flood water go into their house. You can't be the same person in those calls,' he says. 'You come away from that and feel that you've been useful and you've been entertaining and you've been informative. The feedback you get is good when it happens – it's an ego trip, I suppose, so if you can satisfy your ego a bit that's great.'

The programmes

As these profiles show, different radio stations demand different skills from their presenters, and the following transcripts from each of their programmes show how they put these skills to work.

Good Morning Scotland: BBC Radio Scotland, 23 November 2000

Item	Presenter		Duration (sec/min)
GTS			
Intro	John Milne	Eight o'clock, Thursday, 23 November – *Good Morning Scotland* from John Milne . . .	5″
Headline	Jane Franchi	. . . and Jane Franchi. The news headlines. Council services across Scotland will be badly hit as UNISON steps up strike action over pay.	8″

Item	Presenter		Duration (sec/min)
Headline	John Milne	The Republican vice-presidential candidate, Dick Chaney, says he is fit to serve despite suffering a mild heart attack.	7″
Headline	Jane Franchi	There are signs that an agreement on curbing greenhouse gases is emerging at the World Climate Change conference.	6″
Headline	John Milne	And the polls are open in what's likely to prove a unique double contest – the Glasgow Anniesland by-elections.	6″
Tease	Christine McCormack	Business with Christine McCormack. The National Australia bank is being touted as a suitor for the Bank of Scotland . . . And profits are down at the fashion retailer New Look – it says it stocked the wrong clothes over the summer.	13″
Tease	Jeff Webster	The sport with Jeff Webster. Torre Andre Flo will train with his new team-mates at Rangers this morning after completing his twelve million pound move from Chelsea . . . And there were defeats for both Leeds United and Arsenal in the Champions League.	12″
Intro	John Milne	The news from the BBC is read by Victoria Lauder.	3″
Cue and wrap	Victoria Lauder	Council services throughout Scotland are facing severe disruption again today as the public service union, UNISON, steps up its industrial action over pay . . . Report from Joanne McCaulley. (Wrap with insert from local government association spokesperson.)	1′16″
Copy	Victoria Lauder	Republican vice-presidential candidate says he's fit despite heart attack.	18″
Cue and voice piece		Manual recount of presidential votes in America to continue. John Lang reports from Palm Beach. (Voice piece.)	55″
Copy		Violence in Israel following car bombing.	13″
Copy		Three British people injured in explosion in Riyadh.	14″
Cue and clip		Deal on curbing greenhouse gases may be emerging.	42″

Item	Presenter		Duration (sec/min)
		Telephone clip from Deputy Prime Minister, John Prescott.	
Cue and voice piece		Glasgow Anniesland by-elections. Report from political editor Brian Taylor. (Voice piece.)	47″
Copy		Hospitals in England under attack for spreading infections among patients.	16″
Cue and voice piece		Senior Church figures want a rethink over part privatisation of air-traffic control. Bob Dixon reports. (Voice piece.)	1′05″
Cue and package		Scottish executive confirms that ferry routes will not be decided for a year. Cameron Buttle reports.	1′13″
		(Package with clips from marine superintendent and transport minister.)	
Copy		The death of Caroline Benn.	15″
Cue and voice piece		Former King of Greece hears today whether his property will be restored to him. Rachel Ellison reports. (Voice piece.)	1′02″
		Weather.	18″
Headlines		Repeat of main headlines.	29″
Time-check		Radio Scotland news, it's ten minutes past eight.	2″
Sting + intro	John Milne	The latest travel news now from Gillian Dixon.	6″
Travel news with music bed	Gillian Dixon	Travel news.	54″
Tease + time-check + station ident	John Milne	And travel updates from Gillian throughout the programme. It's eleven minutes past eight now and you're listening to *Good Morning Scotland* with Jane Franchi and John Milne	8″
Cue and package	Jane Franchi	And as we've been hearing in the programme, UNISON will step up its industrial action today . . . Package from Eleanor Bradford that includes actuality from east and west coast, as well as the north of Scotland.	3′46″

....

Item	Presenter		Duration (sec/min)
Live interview	John Milne	Well, Geordie Palmer speaks for Unison on local government matters . . . have you lost the case? Live interview with Geordie Palmer.	4'03"
Time-check	John Milne	Nineteen minutes past eight.	1"
Cue + live interview – studio + telephone	Jane Franchi	And to a totally different subject . . . UK football transfer records look set to tumble later today . . . Rangers have completed the signing of Chelsea striker Torre Andre Flo for a cool twelve million pounds – double the previous Scottish record set by Celtic when they signed another Stamford Bridge reserve, Chris Sutton . . . Joining us now, Steven Morrow, the football business analyst at Stirling University, and on the line from Stockholm, pundit, former Rangers forward and agent Gordon Smith . . . Live three-way interview.	4'50"
Time-check	Jane Franchi	It's twenty-four minutes past eight.	1"
Intro	John Milne	And that takes us very neatly to the sports desk manned by that stalwart Jeff Webster (laughter JW) You must have a benefit match coming up soon, d'you not?	7"
Cue + live telephone interview	Jeff Webster	No million-pound transfer here I'll tell you . . . (laughter JM and JF) . . . not twelve million anyway. At a stroke, as you've just been discussing, the Scottish transfer record will be doubled today . . . Live telephone interview with Jim Duffy, well known within the Scottish game as a player and manager, and who's now on the coaching staff at Chelsea . . .	2'20"
Three linked copy stories + cue and clip	Jeff Webster	Rio Ferdinand meets Leeds United chairman to discuss 18-million-pound move to Elland Road. Leeds were beaten last night by Real Madrid in Champions League . . . Other game in same group, Anderlecht beat Lazio one nil.	1'19"
Three update		Arsenal lost four one to Moscow Spartak in Russia.	

Item	Presenter		Duration (sec/min)
lines		Clip from manager Arsene Wenger. Bayern Munich beat Lyon one nil. Third-round first-leg ties in UEFA cup tonight . . . Airdrie lost three one to Clyde.	
Time-check	Jane Franchi	Thanks very much indeed, Jeff . . . twenty-seven minutes past eight.	4″
Cue + live interview	John Milne	A medical pressure group's calling on the government to put money into getting people who fall ill back to work as quickly as possible . . . Live interview with president of British Society of Rehabilitation Medicines, Dr Andrew Frank.	3′20″
Time-check	John Milne	It's just after half past eight . . .	1″
Sting			6″
Intro	Jane Franchi	And Gillian Dixon has all the latest travel	2″
Travel news over music bed	Gillian	Hello again . . .	6″

The *Jo and Twiggy Breakfast Show*: Trent FM, 5 December 2000

Item	Presenter		Duration (sec/min)
Intro + news jingle	Jo	It's just after eight o'clock – here's Lewis . . .	9″
Weather	Lewis Scrimshaw	Wet and windy today, highs of twelve. Now with the latest on our roads, here's Jamie.	5″
Traffic news	Jamie	Traffic news . . .	9″
Sting + music bed.	Lewis Scrimshaw	Curfew orders proposed for under-16-year-olds.	26″
Cue and clip		Clip: 'Tory Home Affairs spokeswoman, Anne Widdecombe . . .'	

Item	Presenter		Duration (sec/min)
Copy		Child-abuse scandal at London school attended by two of Prime Minister Tony Blair's children.	14″
Copy		Good response to appeal for information about last movements of murdered 10-year-old Damilola Taylor.	14″
Cue and clip		Lone parents want more help. Clip from Kate Green from National Council for One Parent Families.	20″
Copy		Abroad now . . . Latest on American election row.	12″
Copy		Back here, a Notts primary school picks up biggest Co-op divie pay-out.	12″
Copy		Nottingham homeless charity needs more money to match anonymous donation.	14″
Copy + time- check		And finally . . . most people hate works' Christmas parties . . . It's four minutes past eight.	10″
Advert		UK Horizon	30″
Weather + music bed	Lewis Scrimshaw	96 Trent FM weather for Nottingham – the world's best city. Wet with heavy rain at times today, strong winds as well, highs of twelve, right now it's eight in Mapperly. I'm Lewis Scrimshaw, next update with Jo and Twiggy at half past eight . . .	12″
Chat	Jo + Lewis + Twiggy	Hey darlin' . . . did you find out about those Christmas lights? (banter between news reader and DJs)	22″
Competi- tion	Jo + Twiggy	If you want to call us 9524040 – we've got a hundred quid to give away . . . Twiggy announces registration of car that has won. Jo – 96 Trent FM.	46″
Music		Madonna – 'Beautiful Stranger'	3′44″
Station ident + chat		96 Trent FM with Jo and Twiggy – it's the morning crew . . . Madonna's 'Beautiful Stranger' today in Nottingham the world's best city high of twelve degrees it's wet and windy and frankly downright miserable . . . but I'll tell you what cheers you up . . .	1′20″

Item	Presenter		Duration (sec/min)
		Discussion about Christmas lights with Twiggy.	
phone number	Jo	952 forty-forty.	
Live call		Discussion about Christmas lights that never seem to work with woman whose husband works erecting them.	1′16″
Advert		Sony Centre store	40″
Music		Robbie Williams and Kylie Minogue: 'Doing it for the Kids'.	3′35″
Station ident + time-	Jo	96 Trent FM with Jo and Twiggy – it's the morning crew – seventeen minutes past eight.	1′04″
check + competition		Mention of school Christmas Fair on tonight. Asks workers to fax them if they would like to have their office decorated for Christmas by them. Twiggy reads out some faxes already received and gives fax number. Winner announced at twenty-to-nine this morning.	
		Jo – it's 96 Trent FM.	
Adverts		Handbag dot com. One-to-one mobile phones. Sports store. Clinical trial people needed. Furniture store.	2′30″
Station ident + time-check + link	Jo	96 Trent FM with Jo and Twiggy it's twenty past eight and our traffic news now every fifteen minutes here's Tony on Thunderbike One	8″
Traffic news	Tony + Jamie	Telephone report from motor-bike rider. Studio report with other traffic news + free phone number for listeners to call in with information + sponsor's name check.	1′20″
Advert		McDonalds	40″
Trail + station ident jingle		Trail for mid-morning show. Jingle for Jo and Twiggy and Trent FM.	35″

Item	Presenter		Duration (sec/min)
Music		Bryan Adams, 'Cloud number nine'	3'32"
Station ident + time-check + phone call + give-away	Jo	96 Trent FM with Jo and Twiggy it's the morning crew – twenty-six minutes past eight. Chat with Twiggy about the Christmas Shopping Network that helps people locate gifts – into call with someone trying to find Winnie the Pooh projector kit. Twiggy announces they have 12 – one for the caller and the other 11 to anyone who phones in.	2'53"
Trail		Trent FM Retro-countdown concert with Deacon Blue.	35"
Adverts		Sony Centre. Window company. Car centre. Shopping centre. Night club.	2'
News jingle		Covering Nottingham like no one else can – 96 Trent FM.	7"
Intro	Jo	It's just after 8.30 – here's Lewis.	2"
Weather + traffic link		Wet and windy today highs of twelve. Now with the latest on our roads here's Tony.	4"
Traffic news	Tony	Telephone report from motor-bike rider	17"

Alan Clifford: BBC Radio Nottingham, 13 December 2000

Item	Presenter		Duration (sec/min)
GTS			
News jingle			12"
Intro cue and clip	Kevin Stanley	It's six o'clock – I'm Kevin Stanley. Democratic presidential candidate Al Gore is due to speak on television when it's thought he may concede defeat. Clip with former White House aide.	47"

Item	Presenter		Duration (sec/min)
Cue and clip		Midland Mainline has promised to offer a near normal service between Nottingham and London. Clip from Midland Mainline spokesperson.	40″
Cue and clip		East Midlands MP calls for help for textile workers made redundant in Nottingham. Clip of MP from the House of Commons.	38″
Cue and clip		Meanwhile there's been implicit criticism by the government of the car makers Vauxhall for the way they have made workers in Luton redundant. Clip of local MP from the House of Commons.	47″
Cue and voice piece		Jury at Nottingham Crown Court told armed police may have chased the wrong motor-bike rider following a shooting incident. Voice piece from Kevin Silverton.	55″
Cue and clip		Severe winds have wrecked a replica Spitfire in Nottinghamshire used to raise funds for charity. Telephone clip with the owner.	44″
Copy		Sports news now . . . Nottingham Forest match tonight is a sellout. FA has charged referee with misconduct following a complaint by Notts County.	28″
		BBC News for Nottinghamshire – our next update is at half past six.	3″
Station ident + traffic news jingle			8″
Travel news	Claire Davie	Traffic delays . . . Further updates until seven o'clock this evening.	1′33″
Sting			12″
Weather	Alan Clifford	Weather for tonight, tomorrow and the next day.	35″
Jingle for Alan Clifford			9″

Item	Presenter		Duration (sec/min)
Cue and live interview		New European Parliament ruling means pictures of rotten lungs have to feature on cigarette packets . . . and other restrictions on cigarette manufacturers. Live interview with BBC Euro Correspondent in Strasbourg.	4'37"
Time-check		It's twelve minutes past six . . .	2"
Station ident			3"
Trail	Andrew David	Sunday breakfast show's letter-writing competition – if letter is read out you can win a pen worth £100.	50"
Station ident			3"
Tease + link into music	Alan Clifford	We're going to be meeting the star of *Whistle Down the Wind* fairly soon . . . after Huey Lewis. Song – 'The Power of Love'	4'11"
Back announce		Song called 'The Power of Love' . . .	10"
Time-check + ident + trail over music + cue into package		It's eighteen minutes past six with Alan Clifford here on BBC Radio Nottingham until seven o'clock this evening after which time we'll have BBC Radio Nottingham Sport's Special . . . Now it's time for our regular Wednesday visit to the theatre in the company of Jo Davis . . . She's been off to meet somebody who's made a bit of a name for himself of late . . .	49"
Feature	Jo Davis	Package with music and telephone interview with the star of the musical *Whistle Down the Wind* showing in London.	8'30"
Intro over music	Alan Clifford	Instrumental music: 'Victory' performed by Bond.	2'43"
Back announce + time-check	Alan Clifford	'Victory' performed by an outfit called Bond . . . It's half past six . . .	14"
News jingle	Kevin Stanley	BBC Radio Nottingham news headlines . . .	6"

Comment

The transcripts from these three programmes show how each one follows a similar format of regular time-checks, travel information and station idents, although the content of each programme is completely different. In each case the content is tailored to suit the time of day and the station's target audience.

The BBC Radio Scotland programme is the most formal in keeping with its role as a serious news magazine show. Nonetheless it uses the same devices as the much lighter *Jo and Twiggy Show* to keep listeners tuned in. The news headlines, for example, not only summarise what is happening in the world, they also act as teases for what is coming up later in the programme. Similarly the teases for business and sports news that have a regular time-slot aim to tempt listeners to stay tuned for the full stories. The programme is punctuated by regular time-checks (seven in half an hour) and traffic news to reflect the needs of listeners on their way to work.

The content of *Good Morning Scotland* focuses on Scottish news with very little reference to other parts of the United Kingdom, although there are several international news stories. This reflects BBC Radio Scotland's role as a national region: much of its appeal is that it gives priority to Scotland in a way the national BBC services do not. The tone of the programme is serious but relaxed and this is emphasised by the light banter between presenter John Milne and the sports presenter Jeff Webster. Although the style of the programme means most items are dealt with in depth, the pace of the programme is maintained by a mix of voices and different ways of telling the story. The UNISON strike story, for example, took up almost eight minutes but it was dealt with through a pre-recorded package that featured views from all over the country and different sides of the story followed by a live studio interview. Unusually the programme did not advertise any other programmes coming up later in the day, and only used a station/presenter name check (ident) once.

At the other extreme, the *Jo and Twiggy Show* on Trent FM had seven station name checks reflecting the programme controller's view that a presenter's first job is to teach listeners the station's name.[8] Like the *Good Morning Scotland* programme, this breakfast show featured regular time-checks and travel news but its style is much more casual. The newsreader, for example, is introduced by his first name only, and he in turn introduces the travel news presenter by his first name. This gives the impression of a friendly team chatting together rather than the more formal Radio Scotland approach. This impression is further reinforced by the banter between the presenters and the newsreader about the city's Christmas lights at the end of the news bulletin, which links in with the 'live' call from a woman whose husband erects the lights.

Even in this brief transcript the identity of the station comes across very clearly: this is a station that caters for Nottingham – 'the world's best city' – and that includes its listeners as much as possible by urging people to telephone or fax them at every opportunity. Its sense of liveness is achieved not only through on-air phone calls but also in the frequent traffic reports that are made from a motor-bike rider on the streets of the city rather than a studio-based report. The show also uses competitions and name checks to keep listeners hooked: even if you do not win the main prize there is a chance your name or that of your workplace may be read out on air. The emphasis for the show to connect with the audience through 'chat' is further underlined by the fact that in this half-hour segment only three music tracks were used.

Nonetheless the identity of both Trent FM and BBC Radio Scotland comes across quite clearly from both these shows – one as a chatty fun station and the other as a serious news programme. As the transcript of his show illustrates, however, Alan Clifford has a less clear-cut identity at the other end of the day. As Alan explained in his Profile, the first hour of his show is strictly news-based but the second hour is less clearly defined combining hard news, arts features and music. This means he has to switch from being a serious interviewer to a chattier DJ in the space of a few minutes. What is clear, however, is that this programme is aimed at an older audience. While the first interview about an EU ruling on the way cigarettes are promoted could be of interest to almost any age group, the arts feature about a London musical is most likely to appeal to older listeners, as are the two music tracks played in the show.

Nonetheless, because this show covers the evening rush hour, it uses a lot of the same devices as the breakfast shows with regular time-checks, weather reports and traffic news. It also has five station idents in the half hour and a trail for the station's Sunday-morning programme.

What the transcripts show most clearly is that while each of these programmes is aimed at a different audience, the same devices are used to try to keep the audience tuned in to that station. As Trent FM programme controller Dick Stone mentioned earlier in the chapter, the job of the presenter is to 'transcend the format' to make it relevant to the audience so that the programme is more than information and entertainment – it is an event that makes the listener feel involved.

Notes

1   All quotations from Dick Stone from author interview, November 2000.
2   This section deals with broadcast scripts in general. For information about writing news scripts see Chapter 5.
3   All quotations from Andy Parfitt from author interview, July 2001.
4   All quotations from Kate Squire from author interview, October 2000.
5   All quotations from Jane Hill from author interview, October 2000.
6   At the time of writing Jane Franchi was working on *Good Morning Scotland*, covering maternity leave for one of the regular presenters.
7   All quotations from Jane Franchi from author interview, November 2000.
8   See comments from Dick Stone at the beginning of this chapter.

5 The role of news

···

T he immediacy of radio means it is eminently suited for the delivery
of news, and the news is an important part of the voice of the
station. Traditionally read on the hour or half hour, the news punc-
tuates programming connecting listeners with the world outside their
immediate environment. However, the days when everything stopped while
the news was read, if they ever existed, are now long gone, and radio
news is now regarded on many stations as just another programme strand
to be tailored to a particular audience in a way that extends the station's
brand values. This chapter examines the way news is used by different
radio stations, how it is selected, and what components make up news
programmes and bulletins. It ends with a brief analysis of two radio news
bulletins to demonstrate how different stations provide a different 'world'
to match the perceived tastes of their audiences.

The importance of news to radio is evident in the different ways it is
used throughout programming on both music- and speech-based stations,
whether as a casual comment by presenters or as the basis of a discussion
programme or a phone-in. But news also has a discrete role in the form
of news programmes like Radio 4's *Today*, *The World at One*, and *PM*
programmes, and bulletins ranging from ninety seconds to five minutes.
As Brian McNair points out, 'broadcasting companies judge themselves
and are judged by the perceived quality of their news services' (1994: 3).

Increasingly, however, the 'quality' of the news is not judged by the
amount of time given over to it or the range of topics covered, but by
the relevance the news is seen to have to the station's target audience.
In other words, the news has become just another product to be tailored
to the station's brand values, that caters to what market research finds the

audience wants to hear about, and how it wants it to be presented. The danger here is that the news will be driven by the market rather than professional journalistic standards and what is presented as 'the news' becomes 'the news our research shows you want to hear'. While critics of this practice say this reduces radio news to the level of entertainment, others claim that matching news to a specific audience is a practice long established in newspapers, and that most people select what news they want to know about by choosing a particular news product.

Most people agree that radio news is at its best delivering breaking stories. Radio programmes are more easily interrupted for a news flash than those of television, and newspapers report what has already happened rather than what is happening 'now'.

However, as a news medium radio has limitations. As Robert McLeish points out, a ten-minute news bulletin is the equivalent to one and a half columns of newsprint and most newspapers carry 30–40 columns of news copy (1994: 5) so the amount of information in a news bulletin is considerably less than can be delivered by newspapers. For this reason radio is often regarded as a summariser of the news, particularly on music-based stations where news output is confined to a few minutes at the top of the hour. As Stephen Barnard comments, 'all too often the analytical ground, the sense of context, is conceded to other media' (2000: 148).

But Andrew Crisell argues that radio gives us an 'indexical' sense of the news through the use of actuality: the sounds – whether background noises like sirens, waves, birdsong, or the way the report is delivered – allow listeners to create the scene for themselves.

> On the radio we hear the noises of the news, or at least the informed view or the eyewitness account 'straight from the horse's mouth' and often on location – outdoors, over the telephone – that newspapers can only report in the bland medium of print, a medium bereft of inflections, hesitations and emphases of the living voice which contribute so largely to meaning, and also less able to evoke the location in which the account was given.
>
> (1986: 121)

The news is an important way for radio stations to connect with their audience, particularly on small stations whose unique selling point is that they are part of the community where they broadcast. 'News is a very good way for us to be local,' says Sheldon James, the station manager at

Oak FM in Loughborough.[1] 'Leicester Sound was the local station here, however they don't have the resources to cover Loughborough in as much depth as we can so it's important for us to have some very strong local angles in our news.'

Even large radio groups use the news to extend their brand and stress their connection with the area in which they broadcast. 'We place a huge value on the news,' says Chris Hughes of the GWR group.[2] 'It's the local core of our "love of life around here" approach. It's critical in giving us local brand differentiation.'

Most local radio stations do not provide 24-hour news bulletins, mainly because it is expensive. Most BBC stations provide hourly bulletins from 6 a.m. to 6 p.m., then provide news on a regional basis until midnight when they switch to 5 Live output. Most commercial stations follow the same pattern of locally provided news until the early evening when news from IRN is taken overnight.

But the popularity of locally produced news bulletins means that for the time being they are unlikely to disappear. 'We could axe our news and it would save us a hell of a lot of money because it's very expensive to do, but the research we've done points to local news being one of the top things people want from local radio,' explains Jane Hill from the Lincs FM group. 'They want local news but they nearly always want three- to five-minute bulletins – they want to be updated but they don't want to be bored. If you can listen to a three-minute bulletin and hear all the national and local news you need to know I think that's a real plus.'

Selecting the news

There are many different factors that influence the production of news from economic and geographical considerations to historical practices that affect the way it is sourced, gathered and disseminated. News is not the 'random reaction to random events' as one journalist put it,[3] but the end result of an institutionalised process that gives precedence to certain topics, events, people and places over others.

These news values vary from one news organisation to another and change over time, but research shows that there are certain factors that consistently influence whether or not a topic is deemed newsworthy. A great deal of research has been done into how some events are favoured over others, most notably by Galtung and Ruge (1981). This has been adapted by many people (cf. Hartley 1982; Allan 1999; Barnard 2000) to show that the following factors are significant in selecting news items:

- *Relevance*: for an event to be reported it must be seen to affect, however indirectly, the lives of the audience.

- *Timeliness*: stories tend to stress what is happening now rather than reflect past events. Events that take place at times when they can be easily monitored are favoured.

- *Simplification*: stories that can be told in straightforward unambiguous terms that are easy to understand.

- *Predictability*: stories that deal with events known about in advance like anniversaries, the release of the latest unemployment figures, or state occasions (diary jobs).

- *Unexpectedness*: something that is unusual or rarely happens.

- *Continuity*: stories where the initial event has repercussions that affect people, as with the fuel protests in September 2000 when protestors issued a 60-day ultimatum to the government and there was a need for regular updates on what was happening.

- *Composition*: news editors like to provide a range of different types of stories in each bulletin so sometimes an item will be included to 'balance' the bulletin to provide a mix, for example of national and local news.

- *Elite people*: items concerning well-known personalities from politics, sport and show business are favoured over 'ordinary' people.

- *Elite nations*: events in 'first-world' countries, especially the USA and Europe, are favoured over those in developing nations.

- *Negativity*: 'bad news' is generally deemed more interesting than 'good news' so stories about disasters, crime and scandal feature highly.

On top of this, in deciding whether or not to include an event in a news bulletin, and what way it should be covered, news editors have to take into account professional and organisational constraints like the availability of spokespeople and the time needed to check information before it is broadcast.

News sources

Journalists get the news from a variety of sources but the most important ones are their own contacts built up over time. These are the people who provide reporters with original stories or inside information that can be used in interviews. Just about every person a journalist meets is a potential source for a story or has the ability to provide information that will lead to a story – from the landlord at the local pub to the local MP. For that reason, one of a journalist's most precious possessions is his or her contacts book which should be backed up either on computer disk or by photocopying at regular intervals so that if it gets lost it is not a complete disaster.

However, as the above criteria of newsworthiness demonstrate, news is not as random and unpredictable as journalistic myth would have us believe. Many events are known about in advance and a note kept on them in the newsroom diary. This will include a note of events like the Christmas lights switch-on or St Patrick's Day parades, as well as reminders about the start or end of important court cases, or public inquiries and events like royal visits or MPs opening community centres.

Newsrooms are also fed information through news releases sent to them from a wide range of people and organisations. While the majority of these are either already known about or not of interest, it is often worth noting the contact name, telephone number and email address of the organisation for future reference. It is much easier to access information through a named individual than trying to get it by asking for an anonymous press officer.

As well as the station's own news diary, the Press Association publishes a daily prospects list showing all the major stories they are covering that day, and on local stations this is supplemented with a prospects list from either IRN, for most commercial stations, or RNS (Regional News Service) at the BBC.

Throughout the day local stations are fed audio and text from their national providers. In the days before the widespread computerisation of newsrooms this was recorded on to tape cartridges to be played into the news when needed, as well as on to a reel-to-reel tape that was triggered to record automatically by tone sent down the line so that there was back-up if a feed was missed. Most stations now take the feed directly on to computer where it can be accessed for inclusion in a bulletin when it is needed. Cues and other text are also delivered via computer rather than over teleprinters, and while some stations still prefer to print off the bulletin, others read it directly from the computer screen.

In most cases national and international news on local radio stations is provided by either RNS or IRN. The BBC's RNS is serviced by correspondents all over the world as well as through the BBC network of local stations throughout Britain, who keep it supplied with audio and text which is then sent on a 'circuit' to BBC regional and local stations, usually on the BBC's computer system known as ENPS (Electronic News Provision Service). Commercial radio news providers like IRN, Sky News, Metro Networks and Reuters work in a similar way. For example IRN, which is owned by ITN, has access to all ITN material, and ITN reporters can supply audio versions of their stories. These are then sent in the same way as at the BBC, via satellite to newsroom computer systems or other automatic recording points.

Another important source of news is the emergency services. Police, fire and ambulance services are usually contacted every couple of hours to make sure any incidents are found out about as soon as possible. In larger towns and cities these services usually have a 'voice-bank' which is a taped version of what is happening updated throughout the day, although not as often as reporters would like it to be.

Similarly, the courts and councils are a regular source of news, although it is not common for radio reporters to attend their proceedings. Recording for broadcasting in courts and at council meetings is forbidden, although some courts will allow dictaphone-style recordings to be made provided the tape is surrendered to the court at the end of the day. Generally the actual sittings are covered by freelance 'stringers' who send their copy to the station where it is turned into copy or a voice piece to be included in bulletins. However, if the council is making an important decision, for example raising the council tax or pushing through plans for a road against the wishes of residents, a reporter may be sent to the meeting to hear the decision, then get interviews with councillors and protestors. Similarly, if there is a major court case going on involving a particularly brutal murder or a case of major fraud, reporters can be sent to hear the sentence and then try to interview the victim's family or those affected by the fraud about how they feel about the verdict. These interviews should be done outside the court buildings.

Like all journalists, radio news staffs also use other media to keep track of what is going on both nationally and locally. Most stations monitor the output of other radio stations in their area, as well as local television, and keep a constant check on Ceefax and Teletext. Local newspapers also provide ready-made stories for reporters to follow up but these should still be checked before being run. It is not unheard of for newspapers to get a story wrong and reporters need to verify information for themselves before broadcasting anything.

The Internet

The Internet is also increasingly being used as a source of information but it has to be treated with a degree of caution. Generally, information from official sites such as those of the government or registered charities is quite reliable, but in most cases it is best to check any information from the Internet through another source. That said, the World Wide Web allows journalists access to a wide range of databases so facts and figures can be checked quickly. Most newspapers are also produced on the web and they often allow access to their archives, which is useful for background information on running stories. Also all the major news organisations have web sites that are constantly updated.

But the Internet should be regarded as a tool for journalists and should not be allowed to dominate working practices. Searching the net can be time-consuming and experts like Randy Reddick, author of *The Online Journalist*, advises journalists to get to know two or three search engines thoroughly and learn their capabilities. Search engines like Yahoo, UK Plus, Alta Vista and Infoseek, generally have a news index that links to most online news organisations. It is also relatively easy to link to most government sites through the search engine index.

Apart from the standard sites like those for the BBC (www.bbc.co.uk, ITN (www.itn.co.uk) and the Press Association (www.pressassociation.co.uk) as well as the local newspaper, it is useful to be familiar with the sites for the main political parties, which carry information about all their MPs including contact numbers as well as local party information. The list of useful sites for journalists is potentially endless and needs to be tailored by the individual according to their needs and interests, however the following list has some sites that will be useful to most journalists.

Search engines

Yahoo: www.yahoo.co.uk
Alta Vista: www.altavista.com
Infoseek: www.infoseek.com
UK Plus: www.ukplus.com

Political parties

Labour: www.labour.org.uk
Conservatives: www.conservative-party.org.uk
Liberal Democrats: www.lobdems.org.uk

Other sites

To trace who runs a particular web site, look at www.networksolutions. com/cgi-bin/whois/whois. The site queries the database of registered domains and gives the names, address and telephone number of those behind the site. This is useful in evaluating any information on a particular site. In addition, there is www.amazon.com, the site of Amazon books, the largest on-line book store in the world. From here it is possible to track down recent publications which is another good way of contacting experts in any given field. Once the author and publisher are known, you can then find them by using something like Infoseek. By entering the name of the publisher it is possible to get details including a telephone number, and often a web site and email address.

There is an electronic discussion list for the UK higher education community at www.mailbase.ac.uk. Some lists are moderated or closed but you can browse the archive for ideas, search for people and subjects, and track down UK academics that are experts in their field.

A site created 'by journalists for journalists' to give them help tracing sources online, advice on Internet resources, and briefings on top issues can be found at www.facsnet.org. It also has on-line tutorials on how to use your computer to help with stories.

USUS (www.usus.org) is 'the usually useful Internet guide for journalists'. As well as a description of the history and development of the Internet, and an introduction to various techniques for research, it has useful links to sites of value to journalists.

Newsgroups and listservs are also useful for contacting people. Listservs work via email. Once registered with a listserv group, every message sent to the discussion group is sent to every other person in the group. Newsgroups, or Usenet groups as they are also known, work through a central 'bulletin board'. On joining a newsgroup, access is given to the central server where messages can be read, replied to or posted.

The advantage newsgroups have over lists is that they allow you to dip in and out of the 'discussion' and this prevents your email system getting overloaded. Listservs have the advantage that they tend to be used by the same type of people – for example, lists for those interested in radio like the one run by the Radio Studies Network. This means users get to know each other and the quality of what is being said can be more easily verified.

However, it is impossible to know the level of expertise of those using a discussion group and reporters need to check the credentials of on-line sources in the same way they would check someone they met casually who appeared to have information. A list of discussion groups is available at Dejanews (www.dejanews.com).

The bulletin

Radio news bulletins vary in duration from 90 seconds on some commercial stations to 10 minutes on some BBC stations. Unlike longer news programmes, their function is to summarise events and bring the audience up to date with the latest events, and this means any analysis pieces or longer interviews are generally not included. Most feature a mix of local, national and international news covering politics, crime, social issues, entertainment and sport.

On most stations the news is compiled and put into a running order by the newsreader, usually to an agreed format. Some stations, for example, like to end every bulletin with a lighter 'and finally' item, while others insist that the lead story should have audio – either a voice piece or actuality – to stress its importance.

As Crisell points out, while newspaper readers can select the order they want to read items of news, 'on radio, order is both a more and a less rigid matter' (1986: 85). It is more rigid because the listener has no choice about the order of items in a bulletin, and less rigid because it does not always follow that stories are read in order of importance. Generally the item deemed to be of most interest to the audience is read first, but thereafter other factors influence the order. These include the need for a variety of topics with a mix of local, national and international items; a variety of sounds with a mix of voice pieces and actuality along with the news-reader's voice; and whether the duration of an item fits into rest of the bulletin.

However, all radio news is constructed from the same basic components described below.

Copy

Copy is a news story written for broadcast. Copy lines vary in duration from 8 to 35 seconds but in every case they have to tell the whole story in more or less detail. Obviously a short copy line will be no more than an extended headline but it still needs to be able to tell the basic story of what has happened. Regardless of its duration copy should be written in a direct style, abbreviating verbs wherever possible to help the piece flow and sound more natural when read aloud, and using everyday language so that it can be easily understood. Wherever possible copy should be written in the present tense – 'says' rather than 'said' – to emphasis its immediacy. As with all writing for broadcast, punctuation should be kept to a minimum – it is very difficult to express a semicolon orally. The best copy starts with a statement that encapsulates the story then adds detail as it progresses.

Most stations have an on-screen proforma for writing copy, cues and scripts. This will contain information about who has written the copy, what bulletin it was prepared for, and a 'slug' or 'catchline' to identify the story. All this information is important to whoever is compiling the bulletin. They need to know who has written it in case there is a query, and when it was written in case it needs to be updated. Ideally copy should be rewritten for every bulletin, even if nothing has changed, to make it sound fresh to listeners. However, because newsrooms are often under-staffed, in practice it often runs unchanged in several bulletins. Another important detail that needs to be included on all copy, cues and scripts is the duration of the piece so that the total duration of the bulletin can be worked out. On most systems this is done automatically, but where it is not, it can be worked out on the basis of three words per second and included at the end of the copy.

Example of copy line

(Writer) John Smith (Bulletin) 20/11/00: 12 p.m. (Slug) US election

Both the Republican and Democratic parties have been outlining their arguments ahead of a crucial court hearing later today which could finally decide the American presidential election. The Republicans have accused their opponents of changing the rules governing the manual recount of votes in Florida, but the Democrats have again said that every vote matters and that it's the duty of electoral officials to ensure they're properly tallied.

Duration: 23"

Cues

Every piece of audio played on radio must have a cue. The purpose of the cue is to introduce the audio whether it is a report from a journalist or actuality from a demonstration. Cues do not repeat what is going to be heard in the audio; rather they set it up, selling the story to listeners in a way that makes them want to listen to what comes next. There is no strict rule about the duration of cues: they need to be long enough to explain the audio but short enough to keep the listeners' interest. As with copy, they need to be headed with the author's name, bulletin time and a slug that is the same as the one used to label the audio. Along with these details there should also be a duration for the cue, a duration for the audio, the total duration of the piece (i.e. cue plus audio) and the 'out words' – that is the last few words of the piece.

Example of cue

(Writer) Jane Smith (Bulletin) 20/11/00: 11.30 a.m. (Slug) waves

The world's first commercial wave-power station has begun supplying electricity to 400 homes on the island of Islay in the Hebrides. Alan Thompson from the company Wavegen says the sparks fly when water splashes around a nearby cave.

Clip: waves

Duration: 12″
Out words: . . . a generator producing power'
Total duration: 25″

Clips

Clips or cuts are the simplest form of news presentation. They are the best short clip from an interview and can be as brief as 5 seconds. Commercial radio tends to keep clips under 15 seconds, while the BBC prefer slightly longer clips – up to 25 seconds – but this is not a hard rule. The length of a clip should be determined by what is being said in it. Clips should advance the story and illustrate it. For example, the mother of a murder victim might not add any new information to the story through a clip, but the emotion she displays will convey her sorrow more effectively than any number of words spoken by a journalist.

Clips can also be used in a 'wrap' when the reporter literally wraps their voice around the clip. This is often done on reports from Parliament that need more explanation than a simple cue could provide, and including the actuality of the politician speaking adds weight to the report.

In the following example from a BBC local radio station, a 15-second clip with a policeman at the scene of a fire with the noise of the clean-up operation in the background, has been wrapped by the reporter. The actuality from the scene gives the piece colour, while the script provides extra information not included in the clip.

Example of a wrap: cue – read by a newsreader

(Writer) John Smith (bulletin) 20/11/00: 1 p.m. (slug) Safeway

A fire that's closed a Nottinghamshire superstore is being treated as arson. Detectives say the Safeway store in Hucknall was also broken into. John Smith has the latest.

Clip: Safeway
Duration: 44″
Out words: '. . . clean-up operation'
Total duration: 54″

Example of a wrap: script – voiced by reporter

(Writer) Steve Beech (Bulletin) 20/11/00: 1 p.m. (Slug) Safeway

The blaze broke out in the early hours of this morning. Firefighters from three stations were called to tackle the fire at the store on the High Street in Hucknall. A forensic team has been examining the scene. Detective Inspector Tony Webster:

Clip: Webster
Duration: 15″
Out words: '. . . than it actually is'

A spokesman for Safeway said the store suffered bad smoke damage and is without electricity. The cigarette booth was also set on fire. The supermarket's hoping to reopen this afternoon and the firm's drafted in staff from other stores to help with the clean-up operation.

Voice pieces

A voice piece is a report voiced by a reporter either live or pre-recorded. Generally they are used when the story requires more explanation than a copy line could convey, for example at the end of a court case when it is necessary to remind listeners about the background of the case. They are at their most effective when they are voiced at the scene when background noise adds atmosphere to the report. For example, a voice piece from a reporter covering a demonstration is much more effective if the sound of chanting can be heard in the background rather than the dead air of the studio.

Again, the policy on voice pieces varies from station to station. Some stations never use them, arguing that a tightly written copy line is more effective than a voice piece. Other stations like them because they add a variety of voices to the bulletin. The cue for a voice piece sets the story up and also introduces the reporter voicing the piece. Some stations use a standard out cue (SOC) on voice pieces, such as 'John Smith, IRN', while others feel that the reporter being introduced at the beginning of the piece is sufficient.

Vox pops

Vox pops, from the Latin *vox populi* – 'voice of the people' – are created by a reporter going out on the street and recording the opinions of people on a particular issue. The reporter then edits the best replies together in a continuous anonymous stream. Vox pops can be an effective way to convey the general feeling about an issue, but they should not be presented as a representative sample. The reporter needs to select the most lively or best-expressed comments without distorting the general trend, and should aim for a mix of male and female voices unless the topic indicates otherwise.

Getting the right question for a vox pop is crucial to its success. It needs to be brief and easy to understand, and phrased so that a simple yes or no is not possible as a reply. Generally vox pops are best suited to lighter items, for example to get a response to a report that claims blonde-haired people are more successful at job interviews. Here the question should be along the lines of 'What do you think about this report that says blondes are more successful than other people?' rather than 'Do you think blondes are more successful than other people?' which could be answered by a straight yes or no.

Unlike straightforward interviews when the pauses and stammers in a reply can reveal as much as the actual words being said, vox pops need to be quite tightly edited with the best response used first and the second best response used at the end. The reporter's voice should not feature in the finished product at all, so the question that has been asked needs to be worked into the cue.

Reporters need to be careful where they choose to record their vox pops. Interviewing people next to a busy road may add to the piece if the topic is about an increase in city-centre traffic, but you need to be careful that the sound of the traffic does not drown out what is being said by interviewees. It is also important for reporters to obtain permission to record on private property. This includes bus and railway stations, shopping centres and pubs. If it is difficult to get permission to record in these places, it is often easier to stand on the street outside and record people coming and going.

Packages

Most news stories have two sides to them; a package is a way to present both sides of the story in a concise way. Generally a package will have clips from two or more interviews linked by a script that is voiced by the reporter.

The best packages use sound effects and music to bring the piece alive. For this reason it is useful for reporters to record a few minutes of 'wild track' – i.e. the background noise at the interview locations – that can be used as a bed for the reporter's links so that there is no sudden change from the background of a clip to the dead air of the studio. This also makes the package sound more immediate and less sterile than a studio-based piece.

As illustrated by the example below, broadcast on BBC Radio Scotland, packages are a good way to explain a complex story where there are different opinions, or to show how a story affects people in different places. Because there are so many different voices in a package, reporters' links need to be direct and brief to allow the story to be told by those directly involved. The example below also shows how sound-effects illustrate the story and are referred to within the script. These not only add colour to the piece but can also be useful to punctuate it, as when the reporter moves from one side of the country to another using the sound-effect of refuse-collection vehicles as an indication of the change. In this example the sound-effect of the telephone ringing is also used to provide a sense of closure by being used at both the beginning and the end of the piece.

Example of a package: cue – read by newsreader

(Writer) Eleanor Bradford (Bulletin) 23/11/00: 8 a.m. (Slug) Dispute

The local government union UNISON is stepping up its industrial action today with an additional seven hundred council and public-sector workers expected to go on indefinite strike. So far 32 councils have been affected in some way as the union tries to force its employers to increase the pay offer of six point one per cent over two years which has already been accepted by two other unions. But as some areas get their first taste of the strike action today, in other parts of the country the situation is getting critical with uncollected rubbish posing a potential health hazard and disruption to schools affecting pupils' education, as Eleanor Bradford found out.

Package: dispute
Duration: 2'42"
Out words: '. . . haven't got their point across'
Total duration: 3'20"

Example of a package: script – voiced by reporter

(Writer) Eleanor Bradford (Bulletin) 23/11/00: 8 a.m. (Slug) Dispute

FX: telephone ringing 2″ faded under reporter.

The phone rings constantly at Douglas Academy on the outskirts of Glasgow but for three weeks there's been no one to answer it except for the headmaster. It's the worst affected secondary school in Scotland. Nearly all of their non-teaching staff are in UNISON and are out on strike. The chair of the school board, John Harvey, feels no one's taking an interest in their plight.

Clip: John Harvey
Duration: 30″
Out words: '. . . affecting a vulnerable group'

Meanwhile parents are growing increasingly sceptical about UNISON's pay demands as they see their children's education being affected.

Clip: vox pop with parents.
Duration: 20″
Out: '. . . my child's education is at stake'
FX: Refuse collection truck faded under reporter – 2″

Meanwhile on the other side of the country people keep putting their rubbish out but no one comes to collect it. Around three thousand tons of refuse has accumulated in three weeks in Mid and East Lothian and there are fears that it's rapidly becoming a health hazard.

Clip: vox with householders
Duration: 25″
Out: '. . . rats and vermin in the place'
FX: Sound of digger machines at a tip – 2″ faded under reporter

As responsible householders there get used to making the trek to one of the few dumps in the Lothians that remain open there are warnings that the north of Scotland will feel the effects for the first time. Moray council is expected to be particularly badly hit – UNISON branch secretary Ken Matthews.

Clip: Ken Matthews
Duration: 25″

Out words: '. . . negotiated outcome'

Conciliation talks with ACAS are still scheduled to go ahead this week
. . .

FX: phone ringing played under reporter.

. . . but while the headmaster continues to man the phones at Douglas Academy exasperated parent Anne Fisher warns UNISON to think carefully about its tactics.

Clip: Anne Fisher
Duration: 9″
Out words: '. . . haven't got their point across'

Telephone clips

As the quality of telephone lines improves, telephone interviews are increasingly common. Their chief advantage is that they get the story 'from the horse's mouth' on-air quickly, and they are particularly useful if the subject of the story is in a remote or far-away place. Most studios have a facility for telephone interviews to be recorded directly on to a computer and edited from there, which not only diminishes the amount of sound degradation but also speeds up the turn-around time for getting the clip to air. Both the BBC and the Radio Authority guidelines stress that reporters must tell interviewees in advance that they are about to record the interview and get permission to do so before the recording begins. Ideally phone clips should be used as a holding position until better-quality audio can be obtained, but in practice under-staffed newsrooms often end up relying on the telephone to get clips in preference to sending a reporter out.

Two-ways

Two-ways or 'Q & As' (questions and answers) are popular within news bulletins because they stress the immediacy of the medium. Generally they involve the reporter at the scene of an incident telling the story in response to questions from the newsreader or presenter. Two-ways need to sound spontaneous to be effective but should be planned in advance. Ideally the reporter at the scene, or in some cases in the studio, having followed the story's development carefully, should write a cue for the presenter and suggest some questions to be asked. Although it is possible to script responses to the questions, it often sounds better if the reporter has a note of key facts in front of them and answers the questions in a more conversational style. The questions need to be direct and the replies should deal with one issue at a time to allow the story to unfold in a way that is easy to understand.

Interviews

The actual mechanics of interviewing – equipment, setting levels, locations – are dealt with in Chapter 6 but it is worth examining the approach to interviews at this stage. Longer interviews are seldom used in news bulletins, where a cue and clip is preferred, but they do feature in news programmes. The strength of a radio interview is that it demonstrates *how* questions are answered – whether there is hesitation or aggression – which conveys as much as the actual words being spoken.

The key to a good interview is preparation. Where time allows, reporters should get as much information as possible about the story and check newspaper files and the Internet for background information. In any event it is important that the *aim* of the interview is clear. Is this a fact finding interview, for example following an accident when you need to establish how many people were killed or injured, where the injured have been taken to, how the accident happened, and so on? Or is it an interview when you need the opinion of the interviewee, for example when interviewing protestors to a proposed ex-offenders unit when you need to establish why they object and what they plan to do about it? Or is it a personality interview with an actor or pop star? Establishing the aim of the interview will help you to plan your approach but the Radio Authority's interview guidelines also require reporters to ensure the following points:

- An interviewee chosen as a representative of an organised group is in a position to speak on behalf of other members or supporters;
- Where practicable, whether the interview is recorded or live, the interviewee has been made aware of the format, subject matter and purpose of the programme and the way in which his contribution is likely to be used;
- Where practicable, the interviewee has been told the identity and intended role of any other proposed participants in the programme.

(Radio Authority News and Current Affairs Code)

As BBC journalist Jane Franchi (see Profile in Chapter 4, pp. 72) suggests, making a list of questions is not a good idea because there is a tendency to follow the list rather than listen to what is being said and respond accordingly. However, making a note of key points that you need to cover can be useful so that towards the end of the interview you can check that they have been covered.

Questions need to be quite brief and direct and should deal with one concept at a time: asking about more than one point in the same question usually means that one point will not be answered. Try to avoid asking questions that can be answered by a simple yes or no and try to remember the basic 'who, where, when, why, what and how' that good interviews should cover.

Whether the interview is live or recorded, and where time allows, the opening question should be quite general to put the interviewee at ease. Any 'hard' or probing questions should be used towards the end of the interview when you already have something on tape should the interviewee refuse to answer, but still have time for supplementary questions if needed. And no matter what the attitude of the interviewee is towards you, it is vital to be polite at all times, as the BBC's Producer's Guidelines point out:

> BBC interviews should be well mannered and courteous. They may be searching, sharp, sceptical, informed and to the point – but not partial, discourteous or emotionally attached to one side of the argument. They should not be hectoring or rude, whatever the provocation. Interviewees should be given a fair chance to set out their full response to the questions.
>
> (BBC Producers' Guidelines)[4]

However, courteous behaviour does not mean total compliance. Your job is to ask questions that the audience would want to ask and at times that will include awkward questions. Some interviewees will ask for a list of questions in advance and this should be avoided. Instead, provide an outline of the general area you will be talking about which will allow you more flexibility and make the replies more spontaneous.

Where possible, the location of the interview should be thought about (see Chapter 6 for more details on locations). For example, an interview about the NHS Direct call centre will sound livelier if it is done against the background of calls being answered than the quiet of an office. This means reporters have to set their levels accordingly to make sure the background noise is not overwhelming but the end result is worth the extra effort. Reporters also need to be careful not to record near computers, air-conditioning units or other electrical appliances because this will cause an unpleasant hum on the tape. Similarly, recording an interview in a high-ceilinged sparsely furnished room will make the recording sound echoey. If this is the only place available for the interview, make sure you stand quite close to the interviewee to shield the microphone and help prevent the sound bouncing off the walls. Wherever the interview takes place you need to ensure you are in a comfortable position so that you do not need to change your stance halfway through, as this can cause mike rattle on the tape. Reporters also need to avoid making noises of agreement or encouragement while the interview is going on. These are intrusive when the piece is broadcast so it is better to encourage interviewees by nods and smiles.

Before the interview begins it is best to establish basic facts like the full name and title of the person being interviewed and any relevant dates or hard facts needed for the cue. Asking the interviewee their name and title and any other facts allows you to set your recording level and is a good way of being able to identify the interview later. At the end of a recorded interview make a quick check to make sure it has recorded, but avoid allowing the interviewee to listen back to it – he or she will nearly always want to change something.

News presentation

The style of news presentation varies according to a station's target audience and general programme style. On music-based stations the news is generally only two or three minutes long, so copy and clips are kept short and the delivery is quite fast. In contrast, BBC local radio and speech-based stations like Radio 4 tend to have longer bulletins, so more time is spent on each story and the style of delivery is more formal and even-paced.

Most news bulletins start with the newsreader announcing the time, their name and the name of the station, and often even short bulletins begin with a headline to grab the attention of the listener. On music stations it is common for the news to be read over a music bed to try to integrate the news into programming and give it the same overall sound as other output, as Phil Dixon the managing director of Leicester Sound explains: 'We try to make sure the news is really very much a part of the hour as opposed to distinct from it, so the news is presented in a similar style to the previous 59 minutes. The presentation style, the content and the packaging are important to get right – we don't want our listeners switching to another station that might not have news at that time – we don't want them switching off because they find our news boring.'

Supporters of selecting the news according to an audience profile say they are giving listeners news they want to hear about rather than what journalists think they should hear about. But this can mean that listeners to one station will get a completely different view of what is happening in the world from those of another station.

Below are transcripts from BBC Radio 1 and Radio 4 bulletins that illustrate the different style and content used by each station. Even without knowing that music-based Radio 1 targets 15–25-year-olds and speech-based Radio 4 is aimed at over 45-year-olds, it is clear the bulletins are designed for different audiences.

BBC Radio 1 News Bulletin: 20 November 2000, 11.30 a.m.

Reader (introduced by DJ Simon Mayo): Andrew Fletcher

Item	Topic	Duration (sec)
Headline	Women are more likely to die from ecstasy	3
Ident	Radio One – Newsbeat	2
1	Report claims women in their teens and twenties are more likely to die after taking ecstasy than other people. Voice piece from Rachael Lawson	29
2	Terrorist group admits planting bomb that killed 2 and injured 12 people in the Gaza Strip.	8
3	American presidential election row over voting.	11
4	British troops to form part of a European Rapid Reaction Force. Clip from army commander on how this will affect the armed services	25
5	Nineteen people injured in bus crash in the West Midlands.	8
6	World's first wave-power station makes electricity in the Isle of Islay. Clip from company director about how it works.	24
7	Bradford City football club name their new manager.	8

Item	Topic	Duration (sec)
Sting + tease	And in an hour's time more on those ecstasy findings, and we're on the trail of the first 'Millionaire' winner on ITV. That's on Newsbeat with Caroline Atkinson at 12.30.	8

BBC Radio 4 News Bulletin: 20 November 2000, 12 p.m.

Greenwich time pips. Newsreader not introduced.

Item	Topic	Duration (sec)
Intro	BBC Radio 4 FM – the news at noon.	3
1	European defence and foreign ministers meeting in Brussels to discuss the formation of a Rapid Response Force. Clip with Foreign Secretary, Robin Cook.	47
2	American presidential election row over votes.	23
3	World leaders meet to discuss how to reduce greenhouse gas emissions. Voice piece from environment correspondent.	53
4	Truck drivers in Australia begin fuel depot boycotts.	19
5	Israel threatens retaliation for bombing on Gaza Strip. Clip with Israeli government spokesperson.	45
6	China and the UN to sign a human rights agreement.	25
7	Gateshead Millennium bridge put in place.	18
Out words	'. . . BBC Radio 4 News'	2

Comment
....

The Radio 1 bulletin was just over two minutes long, while the Radio 4 bulletin was four minutes, but both covered seven stories each. Predictably the Radio 1 bulletin was read at a faster pace than that of Radio 4, and copy, cues and clips were all much shorter.

Radio 1's top story about young women being more at risk from using the drug ecstasy has particular relevance for its target audience of 15–25-

year-olds, and while it could be argued that older listeners might be interested because many of them will have daughters in that age group, the Radio 4 bulletin ignored this story.

In general the Radio 4 bulletin focused on policy-making with four of their stories referring to meetings between world leaders and other politicians, while Radio 1's bulletin generally focused on how events affect people. This can be seen in the different way each station covered the proposed creation of a European Rapid Response Force. Radio 4 referred to the meeting of European defence and foreign ministers to discuss details of the proposal and had a clip with Foreign Secretary, Robin Cook, while Radio 1 only mentioned the meeting in passing and focused on the effect it will have on the armed forces through a clip with an army commander.

As well as stories being selected because of their suitability for the target audience, it is clear that the criteria given at the beginning of this chapter also come into play. For example, both bulletins ran the story about votes being recounted in the American presidential election. This matches the criteria for reference to 'elite nations' as well as 'continuity' in that it was an ongoing story. The inclusion of the item about the Gaza Strip bombing may also have been for similar reasons: it is unlikely that a similar bombing in, for example, Liberia would have been mentioned.

Although the Radio 1 newsreader did not announce himself, he was introduced by the DJ with scarcely a pause before the headline was read. This effectively brings the news bulletin into the programme, an impression that was reinforced by the fast-paced delivery over a music bed, the use of a station ident, and a sting before the tease that advertised what was coming up in the longer 12.30 p.m. news.

In contrast, the Radio 4 bulletin was preceded by the Greenwich Time Signal that signifies tradition and calm. The newsreader was anonymous and delivered the news in an even-paced formal manner underlined by silence of the studio and the lack of headlines and jingles.

But although these bulletins are different in both content and style, they share the same basic characteristics. Both have a mix of copy, actuality and voice pieces; they start with the story deemed most interesting to their listeners; and both end with a lighter item.

Notes

1   All quotations from Sheldon James from author interview, October 2000.
2   From author interview, August 2000.
3   Quoted in Michael Schudson (1996: 141).
4   Available at www.bbc.co.uk/info/editorial/prodgl/index.shtml.

6 The tools of broadcasting

....

The simplicity of radio is one of its greatest assets. At its most basic, all it requires is a microphone and a transmitter to take to the airwaves, although even the smallest stations have considerably more equipment than that. The purpose of this chapter is not to provide a comprehensive list of the equipment used in radio, but to explain how certain key pieces are used to produce the sophisticated sound we all take for granted when we switch on the radio.

Since the mid-1990s the tools of radio have been revolutionised by computerisation and on most stations audiotape, once the most heavily consumed item in radio, no longer exists. However, some older stations still use a mix of old and new technology and even in state-of-the-art stations there are remnants of the past tucked away in the corner of studios, kept more for sentiment than any practical use. For this reason, and to show how technology has simplified broadcasting, some pieces of older equipment will also be explained.

The studio

....

The obvious starting point for any explanation of the equipment used by radio is the studio. This is the hub of the station and it is from here that what we hear is broadcast. Most stations have one main studio from where the majority of programming is broadcast. Generally these are self-operating studios driven by the presenter, but sometimes there is also a facility for the output to be driven by a technical operator who operates the desk in a section sealed off from the studio with sound-proofed glass and linked to the presenter by a talkback system. Stations usually also have at least one other studio that can be used for production work, and a news studio used for broadcasting the news and recording items like voice pieces and links for packages. In the past radio studios were sometimes lavish affairs large enough to hold a small orchestra comfortably. These days most studios are the size of the average bathroom, and news studios can be as small as a large cupboard.

The key piece of equipment in a studio is the desk. This is the control panel that links various pieces of play-out equipment to the transmitter for broadcast. Although a studio desk can look intimidating with rows of sliding faders and various flickering meters, it is essentially very simple. Each fader is connected to a particular piece of equipment. For example there will be a fader for each microphone in the studio, one for the computer, one for each CD or minidisc player, each telephone or ISDN line and so on.

Digital desks have fewer faders with each fader assigned to several pieces of equipment. For example, a desk may have only four faders with each fader capable of connecting to four different pieces of equipment. The presenter then assigns each fader to the piece of equipment they need at that particular time. The desk looks less complicated because it has fewer faders but it works in the same way as an analogue desk.

The meters on desks are visual indicators that monitor sound levels. There are two systems of monitoring sound levels: VU (volume unit) and PPM (peak programme meter). The VU scale indicates the average recording or playback levels, while the PPM measures the peaks of sound. One way to think about the difference between VU and PPM is to think that the average height of the Himalayas is 18,000 feet, while the highest peak, Mount Everest, is 29,035 feet. A VU reading of the mountain range would give you a readout of 18,000 feet – the average height – while a PPM reading would be 29,035 feet – the highest peak.

Radio stations have pre-determined levels where output should peak to ensure an even level of sound. If levels fluctuated too much, listeners would have constantly to adjust the volume on their sets, but there are also technical reasons for maintaining consistent levels. If the level is too low the transmitter will attempt to boost it artificially and this can cause 'hiss' on the output; if they are too high the sound becomes distorted and difficult to understand.

In order to allow the level of any output to be adjusted before it is played out, desks have a 'pre-fade' facility that allows the presenter to hear the source through headphones and set the fader at the correct level. Before doing a live studio interview, for example, the presenter will usually adjust the level on the guest microphone on pre-fade to take account of the interviewee's voice and make sure that both microphones will be heard at the same volume. In theory anything played off a computer should not need to be adjusted on pre-fade because it should all be put into the computer at the prescribed level. In practice, however, this is not always the case and wherever possible even items on the computer should be checked before being broadcast.

Headphones or 'cans' are part of the uniform of all radio broadcasters. They are needed not only to set levels on pre-fade but also to keep the presenter in touch with other people and hear the station output. Most studios have speakers in them that play the station output but as soon as the microphone fader is opened the speakers cut out and the output is heard through headphones only. Headphones also allow presenters to talk off-air to producers or technical operators through a talkback system, and they link them to external sources like telephone callers or traffic-news centres connected by an ISDN line.

Traffic and travel news

These are an important part of radio output particularly on local stations. They provide a service to listeners and at the same time reinforce the station's links with the community by referring to local routes and public service travel operations. Many stations feature traffic and travel news in regular slots every 15 minutes during breakfast programmes and drive-time, and hourly at other times of the day.

Stations draw upon a wide range of sources for their traffic information. Most have an agreement with services like AA Roadwatch or Metro Networks that link their own announcers to the station via ISDN lines. Some stations work with local authorities that use their network of traffic cameras to report on traffic congestion, and utility companies provide advance warning of any road works they are planning in the area. On top of this, stations often encourage listeners to phone in with information about any delays they are experiencing, and some employ helicopter reporters or motor-bike riders to cruise the area on the look-out for hold-ups.

Studio computers

The studio computer has replaced quite a lot of traditional equipment although some studios still have remnants from the past as back-up. Most music, for example, is stored on the computer hard drive and accessed by mouse, keyboard or touch-screen. But even in the most up-to-date studios there are still CD, cassette and minidisc players to supplement what is stored on computer, as well as a television to monitor Ceefax and Teletext. These are arranged around the studio desk within easy access of the presenter.

Pre-recorded material from news packages to adverts, jingles and station ids are also stored in the computer. This means that large open-reel tape-players have virtually disappeared and cartridge players, while still around, are seldom used.

Cartridges, or 'carts', are small plastic boxes containing a loop of tape in varying lengths which can be used for jingles and adverts as well as news clips and features. When a recording is made on to a cart, a 'pulse' is put at the start and end of the recording. The cart machine automatically finds the start pulse at the beginning of the recording and at the end the end pulse will automatically stop the machine and fast forward to the end so that it is ready to play out again. Before computers this was useful, particularly in news bulletins, because it saved the presenter from having to manually line up the start of a piece on a reel to reel tape-player. That said, 'cart failure' was not uncommon, either because the cart had not been fast-forwarded to the beginning or because the tape inside had become worn out through over-use – something there was no way of knowing about in advance.

Another disadvantage of carts is that they do not erase themselves so have to be 'cleaned' before every use. This is done with a bulk eraser which is a box that uses strong electromagnets to destroy all the magnetic patterns made by recording on tape so that it can be reused. The demise of tape in radio means bulk erasers are seldom seen any more.

Outside sources

Studio desks are also linked to telephone and ISDN lines. When a call comes through to the studio the presenter can put the caller on-air by opening the telephone fader on the desk. The presenter hears the caller through headphones, and talks to them via the studio microphone.

Putting the public directly on-air can have risks in that someone could deliberately abuse the situation by using obscene language or inadvertently committing libel or contempt. Because of this the Radio Authority recommends that all phone-ins or programmes that allow the public direct access to air should be broadcast using a delay system known as 'in profanity' or 'prof'. This works by putting the live output through a digital delay unit that provides a delay of up to 10 seconds. In the event of someone saying something that is not suitable for broadcast, the presenter can then press the prof button and a jingle plays over the offending call. The delay at the start of the procedure is covered by playing a jingle, usually automatically triggered via the studio computer.

Most commercial radio stations use prof for longer phone-in discussion programmes, though BBC local radio seldom does (see Chapter 7 for a fuller discussion of phone-in programmes). For shorter phone-in requests slotted into music programmes most stations now pre-record the call on computer, often editing them to make them sound better, then they are played 'as-live'.

Some music stations believe that having callers on-air increases their ability to connect with their audience, but others believe it breaks the one-to-one relationship presenters have with listeners. At these stations presenters still take phone calls from the audience between music tracks or during ad breaks, but instead of putting the listener on-air, the information is passed on to the audience by the presenter.

Connecting to an ISDN line is done in the same way as connecting to a telephone line. The number is dialled from the studio, and once the connection is made, the relevant fader is opened and communication is carried out via the studio microphone and headphones.

The newsroom

Computerisation has also radically changed the way radio news is gathered and disseminated. Once a hotchpotch of huge reel-to-reel editing machines, tapes and teleprinters spewing endless material, newsrooms are now clean tape-free zones with computer work stations that allow journalists to write copy and cues, edit material, access wire services and archive material, research stories and contact sources all from the same terminal.

The big advantage of work stations is that they cut down on the use of studios. In the past a reporter would edit their material on a reel-to-reel Revox or Studer machine. This involved marking the tape with a chinagraph (wax) pencil to show where you wanted to make cuts, physically removing sections that were not needed, and joining the tape up again using splicing tape. A careless edit meant reversing the whole process to get the original back (plus splicing tape) and starting again. The clips for a package then had to be either put on carts or banded on one tape using coloured leader tape to show the start and end of each clip. The reporter then had to go into a studio to mix the clips with links, taking care to line up banded tape so that each one played at the start of the audio. Understandably there was often a queue of reporters waiting to use the studio as the deadline for a news programme approached.

In contrast, work stations allow reporters to edit tape digitally, adding music or sound-effects as they are needed. Links can be added by recording them in a studio and sending them to the work station for mixing, or, if the newsroom is quiet enough, they can be recorded directly on to the computer using a headset microphone. This not only makes news production faster, it also produces a better-quality product because it cuts out the sound degradation associated with rerecording.

Editing

Very little pre-recorded material goes on-air without at least some editing. The most basic edit is a 'top and tail' when an interview runs unedited except for its beginning and end to ensure it starts and ends cleanly when it is played out. But generally material needs more work than this either to get rid of unwanted material that is irrelevant, or when there is not enough time to use it all, or when it is just plain boring; or to rearrange material so that it has more impact, with for example the answer to the third question coming before the first and second, or to make sure the best clip is used first in a vox pop even though it was recorded last.

But whatever the reason, editing should not be used to change the sense of what has been said or put it in a different context by, for example, editing a response to one question on to another question. Not only is this unethical but in some cases it can lead to legal action if the interviewee feels they have been misrepresented.

The Radio Authority offers the following advice for editing interviews:

- A shortened version of an interview must not misrepresent an interviewee's contribution. An interview should not be edited so as to appear by juxtaposition to associate a contributor with a line of argument which he would probably not accept and on which he is given no opportunity to comment in the programme or feature.

- Due weight should be given to any qualifying remarks that may perhaps weaken the force of an answer but to which the interviewee is likely to attach importance. There is no justification for picking out a brief extract to support a particular line of argument to which the interviewee does not himself subscribe without qualification.

- The context in which extracts from a recorded interview are used is important. It is quite defensible to run together a number of different answers made by different contributors to the same question.

- There is no general obligation to offer a pre-audition of the edited version of those whose contributions have been used. On the other hand, it is possible that particular circumstances will make pre-audition by an interviewee desirable or even essential, and producers, interviewers and/or managements should always give thought to this before completing their programme or feature. To minimise the risk of misunderstanding, or even resentment, it may be helpful if the producer or interviewer tells the interviewee that the edited version of his words used in a programme or feature is likely to be shorter than the recording made at the time.

(News and Current Affairs Code)

Whether editing on analogue tape or digitally, it is important that the joins are not heard. As Linda Gage advises, 'Try to match natural speech rhythms as far as you can, which can mean leaving in the thoughtful pause or an intake of breath. Taking out every single breath can make people sound like automatons' (1999: 12).

The aim should be to achieve a natural-sounding piece that flows well with a strong start and a memorable end. A certain amount of 'cleaning-up' of an interview by removing awkward pauses or places where the interviewee has become tongue-tied is acceptable, especially at the start of a piece when many people respond to a question with superfluous words like 'well now, let's see . . .' before getting to the point. But removing all hesitations and pauses can also remove the drama from what is being said. Radio is about voices, and the *way* something is said is often as important as the words being used. As Martin Shingler and Cindy Wieringa point out, pauses and hesitations are particularly prominent in political interviews: 'Here the producer can use such moments to suggest uncertainty, incompetence or, particularly, dishonesty' (1998: 98).

Digital editing

There are many different digital-editing software packages available but they all work on the same principles. The audio is transferred to the computer screen where it appears as a visual representation of the sound known as a waveform. This shows the peaks and troughs of the recording, and you edit by moving the cursor to the beginning of the piece you want to cut out, highlighting the section and then pressing the delete button so it disappears. Most systems allow sections of the waveform to be enlarged by zooming in on it and this allows very accurate editing.

The system is very similar to the cut and paste facility on word-processing packages. Its main advantage is that no matter how many edits you make, the original recording remains intact, so a careless edit can be corrected more easily and there is no degradation in the quality of sound.

Most systems used in newsrooms like CoolEditPro and DAVE in commercial radio, or Radioman at the BBC, have at least two sound channels, and most usually have four. This allows reporters to add sound-effects or music to packages, by recording them on to the different channels and mixing them together at the appropriate levels. It is possible to add music and effects to a single channel editing system, but it is easier if each sound source has a separate channel that can be individually adjusted before being brought together for the final item. Once the piece is completed it is saved in a named file and stored in the appropriate news file.

Most news editors agree that digital editing is faster, easier to use and produces better quality audio than the analogue system. But because it is a visual process as well as an aural one, there can be a tendency for every gap in the waveform to be edited out, which can make speech sound very stilted and unnatural. Reporters need to trust the way a piece *sounds* rather than how it looks on screen and apply the principles of analogue editing to the digital system.

But computers are used in newsrooms for more than digital editing. They are also used for writing copy and cues, collating bulletins, researching stories and receiving audio and text from outside sources.

The BBC is committed to computerising all its regional and local radio stations by 2002 using ENPS (Electronic News Provision Service) and Radioman. ENPS is the system that connects all BBC newsrooms with each other. Each local and regional station and each national news programme has its own folder that can be accessed through the system, allowing news editors in Bristol, for example, to see what stories are being covered in Newcastle, and if it is relevant they can then request the audio and cue to be sent to them on an ISDN line, although eventually it will be possible to retrieve the audio through a computer file number.

ENPS also connects newsrooms to various wire services like Reuters and PA as well as the BBC's Regional News Service that sends what used to be called 'rip and read' summaries of the day's top stories along with other copy and cues. To make sure relevant stories are picked up, news editors list key words to be picked out on each service – usually the names of relevant towns, MPs, sports clubs, etc. – and when those words appear the story is flashed on to their computer screen for them to check.

In fully computerised newsrooms, the regular audio feeds from London (see Chapter 5) are sent via satellite to the station's main computer and stored there. They are retrieved when needed, topped and tailed ready for use, and stored on the newsroom system called Radioman. Radioman is the digital editing system used in the BBC. It also allows reporters to write copy and cues and compile bulletins.

Through a combination of ENPS and Radioman the news editor is able to keep track of events nationally and locally from one terminal. The system allows him or her to access work in progress as well as archive material. Every bulletin is stored on computer and is searchable through keywords which makes compiling programmes like the end-of-year review considerably easier, and provides a useful database for background information on running stories.

Telephone and ISDN interviews are also made simpler because they are recorded directly on to the computer for editing. As well as a telephone and ISDN link in the news studio, newsrooms often have other points available. Other audio from radio cars or reporters in the field with access to an ISDN line is also fed directly on to a computer for editing before being stored in Radioman.

Although commercial radio operates different systems, they all work in a similar way with copy, cues and clips prepared and stored on the computer. Some smaller stations may not have access to a full wire service because it is so expensive, but to get around this news editors can keep a check on wire services via the Internet and follow up relevant stories themselves.

Portable recorders

In the past the standard recorder for radio reporters was the Uher. These bulky German-made machines use quarter-inch reel-to-reel tape, and, although noted for their robustness and quality of sound, they are redundant in the computer age and have been replaced by either the Marantz or minidisc recorders.

The Marantz is a professional American-made cassette machine. Although it records in analogue, it is lighter than a Uher but more robust than a minidisc recorder. The Marantz has features in common with most cassette recorders: play and record buttons, fast forward and rewind facility, and a pause button that is particularly useful for vox pops. It also incorporates a speaker to listen back to recordings. Recordings made on cassette need to be transferred to the computer using a special lead before they can be edited.

Minidisc recorders are compact and lightweight and record digitally on to a miniature compact disc. Apart from the improved quality of sound that comes from digital recording, the minidisc recorder allows reporters to make rough edits of their work in the field. By scanning through an interview the reporter can identify what sections they plan to use, mark them up as individual tracks, and erase unwanted material. On return to the newsroom the tracks are then transferred to the computer for fine editing and/or mixing with links and other material, which cuts down on the time needed to prepare items for use. As with the Marantz, audio is transferred from the minidisc to the computer using a special lead fitted with a mini jackplug, or the disc can be put into a special system, most commonly Denon machines, for editing there.

Minidiscs do not have built-in speakers but their output can be heard through earpieces. No matter what machine is being used to record material, reporters should always check that they have a recording before they leave the scene. It may be embarrassing to ask an interviewee to redo a piece, but that is preferable to getting back to base then finding you have no recording and no way of redoing it.

The main disadvantage of minidisc recorders is that they are not very robust. In most newsrooms this is overcome by using special carriers. Apart from providing protection for the minidisc, carriers like the Reporter have a facility for the recorder to be slotted into that extends its battery life and also provides speaker output. While this makes the minidisc about the same weight and size of a Marantz, its advantages are worth the extra few pounds. Indeed, Marantz also produce a professional heavy-duty minidisc recorder with full speaker capacity that is the same size as their cassette version.

Microphones

There are three main types of microphone that each work in slightly different ways so are used in different situations. Generally the technical staff at a radio station will advise where and how each different microphone should be used, and what follows below is no more than a general description of the three main types of microphone.

- *The ribbon microphone*: these mikes are bidirectional and pick up sounds within the range of a figure of eight. They are most commonly found in studios for interviews or discussions, either on a stand or suspended from the ceiling. Sports reporters use a specialised type of ribbon mike called a lip mike that, as its name suggests, has a special bracket on it to allow it to be held against the mouth. Lip mikes pick up nearby sounds and so allow the reporter's commentary to be heard in noisy conditions.

- *Moving coil mikes*: these can be either unidirectional – picking up sounds from in front of the microphone in a heart-shaped field – or omnidirectional – picking up sounds from all around. Mounted unidirectional mikes tend to be used in newsreading studios, mounted on a stand. Radio reporters tend to use omnidirectional mikes.

- *Capacitor mikes*: these mikes need their own power supply from either a battery or the recorder itself. They vary in the way they respond to sound and are most commonly used as tie-clip mikes for longer interviews outside a studio.

The type of microphone used depends on the situation and each situation has a set of procedures that should be carried out before broadcasting or recording to ensure a technically 'clean' programme.

Newsreading

It is the newsreader's job to ensure that the bulletin is broadcast at the correct level and with no other technical flaws. Ideally the newsreader should get to the studio five minutes before the broadcast. In computerised newsrooms the entire bulletin will be on the news studio computer. The newsreader reads the scripts from the screen and 'fires' news clips stored on the computer using either a keyboard, mouse, or touch-screen. However, many computerised newsrooms still prefer to read paper scripts, so the newsreader must ensure they have the complete bulletin with them in the correct order, and in older stations they may also have to take news 'carts' with them.

Once in the studio, the newsreader should position him- or herself comfortably so as to access computer screens or cart machines without moving away from the microphone. Scripts should be held so that when one story is finished it can be placed silently to one side. As mentioned earlier, most news studios use a mounted unidirectional moving coil mike. This should be positioned so that the bottom of the mike is level with the end of your nose to avoid 'popping' caused by 'p' and 'b' sounds. The newsreader should then open the microphone on pre-fade to set the level for his or her voice. The best way to do this is to read the first story in the way you will deliver it live. Your voice should peak between four and six on the PPM level meter.

Having set the microphone level for him- or herself, the newsreader then has to check the levels of the news jingles and all the news clips being used. These should also peak between four and six on the PPM level meter. In most cases the levels on jingles and clips will have already been checked, but you should never assume that the desk has been left as it should have been so it is advisable to check them yourself.

Once the news jingle has been fired, the newsreader should take a deep breath *before* opening the mike to read the first story. Some newsreaders prefer to leave the microphone open throughout the bulletin, especially if the news clips are very short, but the advantage of closing the mike during inserts is that it allows you to take a deep breath, which gives your voice more resonance at the start of the next item.

Interviews

The general approach to interviewing – preparation, handling interviewees, what kind of questions should be asked – is dealt with in Chapter 5. In this section the mechanics of different types of interviews are discussed.

One-to-one studio interview

Whether the studio interview is live or recorded it is most likely that a bidirectional ribbon mike will be used, although often there will be a separate microphone for the guest. On these occasions presenters need to make sure that they and the interviewee are being heard at the same level. Where there are two microphones this is much simpler. With a single bidirectional mike it may mean positioning the microphone so that it is closer to the interviewee – if he/she is softly spoken – or further away – if he/she has a naturally loud voice.

Presenters usually use the time-setting levels to put interviewees at ease by asking general questions – perhaps about their journey to the studio or the weather – that will give a response so that the mike levels can be set. If it is a live interview there may not be much time to do this and it is sometimes advisable to tell the interviewee what area you are going to begin with, so that they can collect their thoughts and give a coherent response to your first question. In any event, once the interview is underway you need to keep checking that the levels are stable. It is not unusual for softly spoken people to suddenly develop a booming voice when they realise they are on-air or being recorded and you need to be alert to this and adjust the levels accordingly. That said, you will get better responses if you can maintain eye-contact with your interviewee, nodding encouragement and smiling appropriately, so the occasional glance at the level meter is all that is needed.

Discussion programmes

Discussion programmes will nearly always use bidirectional mikes but occasionally each participant will be fitted with a capacitor tie-clip mike. Where there is one microphone it should be positioned so that each participant can be heard at about the same level. Where clip mikes are used you need to warn interviewees not to put their hands to their throats when they are talking, as this will obscure their mike and/or cause mike rattle.

Recording interviews in the field

Before going out for an interview you need to check your equipment is complete and working. Recorders should be checked to make sure they are fully charged, and if it is going to be a long interview extra batteries should be taken as a safeguard. Next you need to check that the microphone and lead are working. For interviews being conducted outdoors, microphones should always be fitted with a foam wind-sock even if it is not particularly windy on the day in question – even a slight breeze can sound like a howling gale if it is picked up by the mike.

On arrival the location of the interview needs to be assessed. Most locations outside a studio have some drawbacks that can cause distortion on the recording and you need to be aware of them so that they can be avoided or worked around. Modern offices, for example, can be a minefield because of all the electrical equipment in them. Where the office you are interviewing in has a computer, you should ask if it can be turned off for the duration of the interview otherwise its hum can be picked up by the microphone and sound very distracting when it is played back. Similarly, if there is noisy air-conditioning you need to ask if it can be turned off or find another place to do the interview. Wherever possible you should also ask for telephones to be unplugged or calls to the office stopped.

At the other extreme, large empty rooms with high ceilings and uncarpeted floors also cause problems because the sound bounces off the walls, making the interview sound as if it were recorded at the bottom of a mineshaft. If there is no other place for the interview to be done you need to try to dampen down the reflected sound as much as possible. One way to deal with this problem is to stand in a corner of the room and position yourself and the interviewee in a 'v' shape to trap the sound as much as possible. Where this is not possible, it is worth sitting as close as possible to the interviewee so that your bodies act as a shield for the sound.

In any event, even in the most accommodating setting, you need to be much closer to the interviewee than you would normally be were you simply having a conversation with them. This can be quite intimidating for the interviewee, who may feel their space is being invaded, so sometimes just explaining that you need to be close to them for the recording to work properly puts them at ease. If the interview is being done standing, position yourself at right angles to the interviewee so that you are close but not 'in their face'. Standing directly in front of someone tends to make them take a step back and you can end up literally backing them against a wall which is not the most relaxed way to conduct an interview. If you are sitting down for the interview, arrange the chairs in an 'L' shape so that your knees are almost touching. If the interview is taking place at a desk or table, position the chairs at one of the corners. Never interview anyone across a desk – you will have to stretch too far with the microphone which is not only awkward but risks one of you being off mike. There is also more chance that the mike movement will lead to mike rattle on your interview.

Although reasonably robust, hand-held microphones are sensitive to movement especially where the lead goes into the mike and also where it connects to the recorder. The microphone should be held firmly with the lead looped loosely around your hand. Make sure that the lead connection to the microphone is not too taut and that you are not pulling on the connection to the recorder. The position you adopt for the interview should mean that during the interview there is minimum movement of the mike.

Once in position you need to take your levels. It is important to get your levels right because an interview recorded at too low a level will have to be boosted for transmission and this leaves an annoying hiss on the recording. Interviews recorded at too high a level have distortion on them and often they end up being untransmittable. As with studio interviews, you can use the chat needed to set levels as an ice-breaker by making small talk.

Position the microphone about a hand-span away from the interviewee's mouth – any closer and it becomes intrusive and will be likely to distract them from what they are saying. The microphone should be an equal distance between yourself and the interviewee, unless one of you has a louder voice, in which case you will need to move the microphone until your voices are balanced. It is a good idea to start the recording with the interviewee giving their name and position as this will help you to identify the recording later.

Most recorders allow you to either set the levels manually or use the automatic level control on them. The automatic level control works by keeping the signal below distortion point and boosting it when it falls too low. The problem is that to keep the signal even, the automatic control uses any background noise and boosts it to the same volume as the speech, which causes a 'surging' effect on the finished recording. Manual level-setting produces a better quality recording and gives you more control over it. For example, if you are doing a package about transport systems, you might want to interview a bus operator in the bus station to give the piece a sense of location and some colour. With the recorder on manual you can set your levels so that the bus station noises are in the background and your interviewee can be heard clearly over them. With the recorder on automatic, every pause in the interviewee's speech would be filled with bus noises at the same volume as their speech, which would not only be distracting when it is played back, but also sound very unnatural. Generally, automatic level control should only be used in very quiet, near-perfect recording conditions.

At the end of the interview check that the piece has recorded *before* you leave. There is no need to play the whole thing back, but you should rewind and make sure it has recorded, then express your thanks and leave. It may be embarrassing to have to redo the interview if there has been an error, but getting back to the station with nothing on tape is even worse! Before you leave you should also check that you have the interviewee's details – full name, proper title, and at least one contact number.

Finally, on the way back to the station it is a good idea to listen back to the full interview. This will remind you of exactly what has been said and allow you to do some mental editing so that when you get back you already know what your cue will be and what clips you will use.

The digital age

It should be clear from this chapter that improvements in technology have made radio broadcasting simpler. Getting items to air using digital technology is quicker than the old analogue system and the sound quality is better, but it is still the skill of the presenter or reporter that differentiates good broadcasting from the mediocre or bad.

One disadvantage of computerised radio stations is that because there is more than one system in use, every new recruit has to be trained to use a particular system before they can fully participate in the life of the station – a particular problem for freelance presenters and journalists. However, the principles behind every system are similar enough to mean that being able to operate one makes it easier to understand all the others, and the best advice for would-be broadcasters is that they get a thorough knowledge of whatever system is available to them through repeated use and practice.

The main advantage of digital technology – its speed – means radio output can be more creative in less time with a wider variety of voices and sounds made available to listeners. Radio is about communicating and as the following chapter examines, there are various forms of programming available to achieve this end. The technology behind the process should be used to improve the quality and range of what is being communicated rather than dominate it. It is not enough for the technology simply to make radio broadcasts faster – they should also be better.

7 Types of programming

very radio programme is designed to a particular format that takes into account the time of day it is broadcast, the target audience and the station's brand values. Phone-ins, for example, tend to be scheduled when listeners are likely to have time to participate like mid-mornings, evenings and weekends. Sports programmes usually centre on key sporting times like Saturday afternoons and mid-week night games. Similarly the content of these programmes needs to be of interest to the target audience and in line with the way the station promotes itself. A mid-morning phone-in on a family-orientated station is unlikely to feature 'blind dates – are they foolish or fun?' as its topic, but it would be quite appropriate for a late-night programme that targets a young audience.

This chapter examines two of the commonest types of programmes used on radio – the phone-in and sports programmes. It then looks at the problems around covering elections on the radio, and the way the medium responds to unexpected emergency situations such as those caused by flooding or snowstorms.

Of course there are many other types of radio programmes available but the intention here is to deal with those most widely used. Radio drama, for example, has a huge following, but it is largely confined to Radio 4 and Radio 3 and is very much a specialist area. As those involved in radio drama often observe, the scope of good radio drama is limited only by the imagination of listeners. Radio allows writers and producers to create worlds far more effectively than either television or film and at a fraction of the cost. This is shown by the huge popularity of the now cult radio series *The Hitch-Hiker's Guide to the Galaxy* by Douglas Adams. The television version of the series never achieved the same impact as its radio original, which also spawned a record album, a computer game and several stage adaptations. The ultimate accolade sadly came after Adams's death, as Jenny Gilbert reported in *The Independent on Sunday:*

> On 11 May 2001, the very day that the 49-year-old Adams died of a heart attack, the Minor Planet Centre space agency announced its plan to name an asteroid 'Arthurdent' – after the ordinary-guy hero of *Hitch-Hiker's Guide.* A coincidence, but a charmed one, worthy of the Cyrius Cybernetics improbability drive itself.[1]

Adams's work gave radio drama a much-needed boost but it is still widely regarded as 'the Cinderella of drama', perhaps because it takes more effort on the part of the audience to appreciate it.[2]

The phone-in

Radio phone-ins began in Britain in 1968 on BBC local radio and were adopted by commercial stations when they came along in the 1970s. As phone-in presenter Brian Hayes notes, 'At that early stage they were novel but mostly dull' (1994: 42), partly because producers were wary about allowing the public on air and so kept to 'safe' topics that were unlikely to cause controversy, and partly because listeners were not skilled in how to participate. As Linda Gage points out, 'Over the years callers have come to understand the procedure and what is expected of them. They have learnt to be callers' (1999: 75).

From the beginning phone-ins were seen as a cheap way to fill air-time and for commercial radio, tied to a speech/music ratio by the Radio Authority, they were also an easy way to bring their speech content up to the required level. But it soon became clear that phone-ins also serve other functions. Through the phone-in, a station can create a dialogue with its listeners: the station not only talks to listeners, it also allows them to talk. The phone-in gives people who would not normally be consulted publicly a chance to express their opinion and enter public debate. As Stephen Barnard notes, 'Encouraging listeners to take part in local or national debates is an important reputation-enhancer; it enables stations to underline their own participation in and commitment to the democratic process' (2000: 158).

Just how democratic phone-ins are in practice is another issue. The topic is usually selected by the phone-in producer and presenter, callers are screened before going on-air, and if they deviate from the agreed subject they can be brought back to their point by the presenter or even cut off. Ultimately the phone-in is controlled by the production team with the presenter setting its tone and steering the debate. Listeners are invited to talk on the unspoken condition that they allow themselves to be guided by the phone-in host. Research by the Broadcasting Standards Commission and the Radio Authority (Hargrave 2000) suggests that listeners expect phone-in participants to be aware of how they should behave and what sort of treatment they will receive from different presenters.

> Some participants felt it would be obvious quickly, when listening to a programme, to gauge the style of a presenter . . . If presenters were known for the 'bad' treatment of callers, the caller should accept or expect that they were going to be treated badly. Some participants in the groups even went so far as to say that callers deserved *'everything they get'*. Others felt that if callers telephoned in, then they should be clever or fast enough to *'give as good as they get'*, so they do not open themselves up to mockery.
>
> (Hargrave 2000: 20)

That said, 'shock jock' tactics of ridiculing callers and being deliberately outrageous did not catch on in Britain in the same way as it did in America through DJs like Howard Stern. When Talk Radio (now talkSPORT) first launched in 1995 it featured controversy-making American style phone-ins with presenters like Caesar the Geezer, whose views prompted a torrent of complaints to the Radio Authority. Although his programme regularly attracted 120,000 listeners and generated publicity for the new national station, the style did not have a wide enough appeal and after eight months he was sacked and the station's output was reshaped.

At a local level, however, phone-ins can stress the station's involvement with the community by being able to discuss local topics that might otherwise be ignored, and by featuring local people. This reinforces the perception that local radio is a responsive medium that is part of the community it serves. Most important, however, is the fact that phone-ins are popular with listeners. For those who call in, it is their five minutes of fame, while for others it is a reminder that although they may listen alone, they are part of a wider listening community. As Elwyn Evans put it, late night and through the early hours phone-ins are 'almost entirely a social service for the lonely, especially the insomniac lonely' (1977: 56).

Phone-in topics

The most popular phone-in format features a presenter to steer the discussion along with one or two guest 'experts'. Typically these programmes will deal with topics related to news stories, consumer issues and advice lines. Some programmes, like that of BBC 5 Live's Nicky Campbell, demonstrate the flexibility of phone-ins by debating the big issues around the latest news stories, while others like BBC Radio 4's *Money Box Live*, which deals with personal finance issues, have a specific topic that is known about in advance by listeners.

Karen Morgan, a phone-in producer at 106 Century FM, says that although phone-ins sound spontaneous, a lot of work goes into them behind the scenes. First of all the topic has to be selected. 'I try to choose topics I think people will want to talk about or that they don't get the chance to talk about in other places,' says Karen.[3] 'Sometimes we do things that have been in the news but we try to cover a wide range of issues.' Her late-night phone-in, for example, covers relationship/sex issues and has dealt with bisexuality, homosexuality, HIV/Aids as well as lighter topics such as male escorts and buying the right present for your partner.

The show features presenter Paula White and resident 'agony aunt' Barbara Jacobs, a trained counsellor, who have a studio discussion with a guest before taking calls. 'You have to have the right guest – somebody who is a good talker and won't freeze on-air,' Karen explains. 'It helps to have a good list of contacts and even when I'm reading the newspaper I'm looking for contacts for particular organisations. It's just a matter of networking and using your initiative.'

Karen usually establishes the suitability of a guest on the telephone then meets them before the programme starts to go over the procedure and explain what is going to be discussed and how they fit into the programme. She also briefs the presenter about the guest and supplies a list of points that can be brought into the discussion. 'The presenter has their job on-air – your job is to feed them with the right material so that you get a good show,' she says.

After that it is down to the callers. 'We take people's numbers and call them back,' Karen explains. 'Depending on the show, it can be a bit slow to start and sometimes I'll book calls to get the debate started – contacts from previous shows or other jobs that I've done. You can usually tell a lot about someone just from their voice. I usually ask them to tell me their story and if they're not very clear and it doesn't seem to make sense I don't put them on.'

Once Karen has lined up a caller she puts their name and where they are calling from into a computer linked to the studio for the presenter to read, and briefs the presenter on talkback about the nature of the call and any particular details that need to be drawn out.

Once on-air it is up to the presenter to keep the caller on the subject or cut them off if they become too long-winded. 'Some people go on-air and say something completely different to the story they've told me but there's nothing you can do about that,' says Karen. 'Some people are fine but once they go on-air – because they're nervous – they just sound silly but Paula has no qualms about cutting them off.'

The presenter also has control over the profanity button that allows her to 'dump' callers because they are swearing or saying something that could lead to libel action. Even if the libel is unintentional, the station is respon- sible for broadcasting it, so extreme care has to be taken whenever a caller starts to mention brand names or particular personalities. The profanity button allows the station output to be broadcast with a delay of up to ten seconds so that if a presenter feels the need, she can press the button before anything offensive is broadcast.

Even on stations that do not phone their callers back, the Radio Authority requires all commercial stations to keep a log of callers' names and telephone numbers in case there is a need to contact them later. Where stations do not phone callers back, every effort should be made to get the caller on-air as quickly as possible not only out of politeness but also because the longer people are kept hanging on, the more they are likely to change their mind and hang up.

And despite the nature of the programme, many people who call do not want to go on-air. 'People will phone-in and say they want some advice or they want to speak to the counsellor but they don't want to go on-air,' Karen explains. 'Usually I'll explain that we actually want people to go on-air and, depending on their story, I'll suggest they use a different name or say they're calling from somewhere different to get them on-air.' But in some cases the calls are not suitable for broadcast either because the caller is ranting or inarticulate or because they are too emotionally unstable. 'There have been a few calls from people who are really desperate and threatening to kill themselves and that's really hard,' says Karen. On those occasions she will get the counsellor to call them back off-air with advice and information of help-lines they can contact. 'We always have numbers of help-lines and organisations that can help people with specific prob- lems for every issue we deal with,' she says.

At the other end of the scale, even the best-thought-out programme can fail to get callers. 'It doesn't happen often but you've got to have back-up for when it does,' Karen explains. 'We always have another story lined up or a letter from a listener asking for advice – a lot of our calls are people giving advice to other callers.'

But whether the phone-in is a serious discussion on a news item, one dealing with consumer issues, or one on personal relationships, they all involve listeners directly, and according to Brian Hayes that is their main appeal. 'We like to hear fellow human beings talking, even if they talk a load of rubbish. However, one person's load of rubbish is another's common sense. It is our different perception of what is being said that makes it worthwhile listening to' (1994: 44).

Sport

Sports coverage on radio varies from station to station. For national stations like BBC 5 Live and talkSPORT it is a central part of their output, while the other national stations give varying amounts of time to it. But sport is important to most local radio stations because it provides a focal point for the relationship between the station and the audience. This is particularly true in areas where football supporters are passionate about their clubs, like Scotland and the North East of England. But even in areas where football support is less fanatical, sports programmes attract a loyal audience who can often be won over to other programmes.[4]

On many music-based stations sports coverage is done by news reporters and amounts to little more than a short copy line at the end of the news bulletin supplemented by the classified results on a Saturday after 5 p.m. Other stations take the subject more seriously and have dedicated sports journalists who not only provide material for news bulletins throughout the day but also broadcast special sports programmes on Saturday afternoons, during mid-week night games, and around special events like cricket test matches or major tennis tournaments.

Presenting a sports programme is one of the most demanding jobs on radio. To begin with the audience is generally well informed about the subject and they expect programme presenters and reporters to have an in-depth knowledge. 'You've got to have a knowledge and a thirst for sport because you can't turn to reference books when you're on-air – you've got to know it before you go on-air because the audience probably does,' explains BBC sports journalist Pam Melbourne.[5] 'If you don't get it right the switchboard goes mad and you know straight away you've not got something right.'

Added to this, sports fans are often passionate about the club they follow, and on a local station that covers more than one football team this can mean walking a tightrope to avoid showing preference for any particular team because that could alienate half the audience.

In the North East, Metro Radio covers both Newcastle United and Sunderland football clubs, with commentary on FM for one and AM for the other. The rivalry between the teams is intense, and sports journalist Dan Thorpe says that despite their best efforts they are continually accused of bias by both sides. 'There was one weekend when Newcastle played Sunderland and Sunderland won. Obviously half the people who listen are Sunderland fans and they want you to play it up and say Sunderland hammered Newcastle, but the Newcastle fans just want to forget it and they want you to be a bit low key,' he explains.[6] 'Whatever you do people are going to think "he obviously supports the other team" so it's very hard and you do get a lot of criticism.'

The level of passion about the game can even turn nasty, as when Metro's Sunderland commentator Simon Crabtree jokingly said after the derby match between Sunderland and Newcastle that the Geordies had 'taken one hell of a beating'.[7] This upset Newcastle fans so much that he received death threats and had to take security measures until the furore died down.

But the positive side of sports reporting is that unlike many other radio programmes that are used in a secondary way, the sports audience is attentive and what is being broadcast can have an effect on them. Pam Melbourne says that when she worked in Derby it was said that if Derby County were performing well, production at Rolls Royce went up. And Dan Thorpe admits that since working in the football-crazy North East he has learnt a lot about the passion behind the sport. 'I came from the South East where people are interested in football but it's not everything,' he says. 'Up here if the team loses, people have a bad week, and when Newcastle lost to Sunderland a lot of people didn't go into work on Monday because they couldn't face their Sunderland mates. You realise then that what you're saying really does matter to people.'

As well as covering sporting events and interviewing participants, sports journalists are expected to keep the news desk supplied with fresh copy, cues and clips and packages. Another important aspect of the job is archiving material for use in future shows. For example, if there is a programme on the day of a game between Manchester United and Sunderland, Dan Thorpe at Metro Radio would be expected to go through the station's seven-year archive of games so that key moments from the time they last met could be played into the programme to remind listeners of their performance.

But despite being 'a bit of a scrum', interviewing managers and players is the highlight of most sports reporters' jobs. 'It's usually quite orderly when you're talking to the manager because he's accompanied by a press secretary and you sit down and it's quite civilised,' explains Dan Thorpe. 'But when it comes to collaring the players . . . they turn up at the training ground and they don't want to talk to you, so they try to find new doors to sneak into all the time and you have to chase them around. There'll be five or six different radio people outside the training ground and you've just got to hope that somebody will talk to you.'

Getting interviews after a match is less frantic because journalists are not allowed to follow players into the tunnel, but have to wait outside for a player to be sent out to talk to them. This can often take a long time, particularly if the team has lost. 'You're forever waiting around in sport, particularly at football clubs,' says Pam Melbourne. 'That's the worst part of the job – you pop out to do a quick interview and three hours later come back with three minutes worth.'

It is also not unheard of for football managers to ban radio stations from their press conferences, or refuse to allow players to talk to certain reporters deemed to have been over-critical of the club. For that reason sports reporters have to be more diplomatic than their news counterparts. 'You're on a real tightrope with the questions you ask because football people are notorious for the way they treat reporters and that does affect you a little bit. You know you can't criticise the club or criticise the chairman or manager too much because you need to interview them tomorrow,' says Dan Thorpe. 'In news if you interview someone and they evade the question you would try to pin them down. But in sport if you ask a question they'll sometimes say "I don't really want to talk about that" and you'll have to leave it because they won't answer and the next time you ask them for an interview they'll just walk past you.'

And while it might be thought that this sort of situation could be made worse by being a woman in a male-dominated area of broadcasting, Pam Melbourne says that because more and more women are becoming involved in football – working in the game and reporting on it – this is no longer a real issue. 'There's still some resistance from the old-school hacks, particularly the print journalists, but you just have to learn to live with it,' she says. 'In terms of the managers and players I deal with – they're fine. They accept it and don't have a problem at all.'

With so many foreign players in British football, an added pressure for sports reporters is the correct pronunciation of their names and many new players go through various versions of their name before the correct one is established. 'A lot of the time it's a lottery on how you pronounce names,' says Dan Thorpe. 'If it's a team that you cover then it's your business to know how to pronounce names, but when it's a new player and it comes through on the wire that there's transfer speculation, there's often no one you can phone to find out the correct way and you just have to sound knowledgeable.'

Presentation and commentary

Sports coverage on both radio and television underwent dramatic changes in the mid-1990s when the cost of commentary rights for major sporting events was pushed up by competition between terrestrial and satellite broadcasters scrambling to make exclusive deals for popular sports like cricket and football.

In football, the Football Association (FA) has a dual/exclusive deal with BBC 5 Live and talkSPORT for commentary on all national and international football matches. Other commentary rights are negotiated between individual clubs and radio stations in their area on either an exclusive or shared basis, although news access is free. Commentary rights for other sports are agreed in a similar way with the sport's governing body negotiating with individual stations.

The rise in the cost of commentary rights is shown by a deal between BBC 5 Live and the football Premiership to give the station exclusive rights from August 2001 for three years for a reported £42 million. The station also has rights for the Wimbledon Championships, the Open Golf, the Ryder Cup, the Six Nations and Super League rugby matches, and exclusive rights for Test cricket commentary for *Test Match Special* on Radio 4 LW.

With so much sport tied to exclusive deals, radio stations have had to change the way they cover it. Where previously Saturday-afternoon sports programmes would be based around live football commentary, many stations now have to produce a studio-based programme with regular match reports from important games to keep listeners up to date. Often these take the form of a presenter with one or two football experts who will have a studio discussion and take calls from listeners in between match reports and sports packages. However, unlike news programmes that can be carefully planned, sports programmes have to be able to change direction according to what is happening at the live event. For example, if five minutes from the end of a football match with the station's local team about to win promotion a goal is conceded, the whole tone of the next part of the programme would have to change from one of celebration to disappointment. Presenters have to be able to stay on top of what is happening and be ready to change the direction of the programme accordingly, taking advice from their producer via talkback or the studio computer and all the while adding to and steering the studio discussion.

Despite the pressure, Pam Melbourne says it is still one of the best jobs on radio:

> I find it really exciting to present a programme. You get quite an adrenaline rush and sometimes when you come off from presenting it's quite a low because you've been so pumped up for hours and when it's finished it's finished. You have to have the sort of brain that can take information in all the time because there will be times when you have to fill and you have to be ready to do that. A sports programme on most radio stations starts at two o'clock in the afternoon and it'll finish at say six o'clock. That's a long time to be working without scripts and that's what you're doing.

However, where commentary from a sporting event is possible it shows radio at its best: it is live and reactive, conveying not just what is happening on the pitch but also the reactions of the crowd and the atmosphere of the event so that the listener shares the whole experience. Television may have pictures but for many fans the next best thing to being at an event is listening to it on the radio, a paradox even seasoned commentators like the BBC's cricket commentator Christopher Martin-Jenkins finds puzzling:

> There is no doubt that there is something about sport on radio which holds the attention more than television often can or does. It can only be the scope it allows for the imagination of the listener, although that hardly explains why so many say they like to watch television with Radio 4 commentary on and the television sound off. The peripherals

of TMS (Test Match Special) commentaries are appreciated as much as the technical observations it seems. Not just the buses, the birdlife and the cakes . . . but the infinite byways, cricketing and otherwise, into which commentary often leads.

(Martin-Jenkins 2000: 3)

Whether commentating on a sport or another event, Elwyn Evans (1977) advises lots of preparation so that not only the event is described but also 'associative material' that adds life to the report. As he points out, this information 'won't come out of the top of your head. You can only meet the challenge if you have background information galore' (1977: 159).

At sporting events like football matches a lot of the atmosphere is provided with effects microphones that relay the sound of the crowd, and as well as reporting on the game the commentator has to be aware of the crowd's reactions and explain those to listeners. If the home-side crowd is cheering and the commentator has not said anything to explain why, listeners will realise they are not keeping pace with the game. That said, many fans attending a game will still tune in to the commentary on portable radios to get added information about the play. 'Commentators have to read the game very well,' says Dan Thorpe. 'They'll often say so-and-so's breaking down the right and the fan won't have even picked that up. They'll look and the ball will be passed and that helps them get more involved with the game. They listen for the commentator's expertise.'

As Elwyn Evans notes, 'the commentator's role . . . is to sustain and amplify the sort of monologue which most of us go in for when we watch a game or a great ceremony' (1977: 158). But unlike private monologues, the radio commentator has to speak almost continuously and often completely unaided. 'The best commentators work for two hours without a script,' says Pam Melbourne. 'They'll tell you there's a goal then describe it back to you in detail – and that's without notes because there isn't time to make any. They literally relive the moment.' In so doing commentators not only inform their audience, they also convey the experience of the event to listeners in a more intense form than either television or print can provide.

Elections

Election coverage on radio is such a minefield of restrictions that many music-based stations choose to restrict their cover to reporting that the election has been called and giving the results at the end. For other stations, however, elections are periods of special programming both in the run-up to the day and on the night of the poll. Given the number of elections there are, this can mean doing election coverage of one kind or another almost every year. General elections are held at least once every five years; local councillors are elected for a four-year term: on some councils this means the whole council stands for election once every four years, but others hold an election every year with a third of the council standing each year. European Parliament elections are held every five years; and by-elections can occur at any time.

The broadcast media are subjected to more stringent restrictions during an election period than are the print media. Newspapers can favour certain candidates over others, campaign for certain political parties, and even run the results of opinion polls on the day of polling itself. But under the combined effect of the 1981 and 1990 Broadcasting Acts, the Representation of the People Acts 1983 and 2000, and the Political Parties, Elections and Referendums Act 2000, television and radio must provide fair and balanced election coverage, and keep records to prove that this has been done. Stations and their presenters must never endorse a particular candidate or party on-air. Any infringement of this rule is dealt with severely by the Radio Authority, as in May 2000 when Virgin Radio was fined £75,000 after DJ Chris Evans made two announcements that he was backing Ken Livingstone in the election for the mayor of London.

There are four key stages in an election.

- The election date is announced but the names of the final candidates are not known. The election is now said to be pending.
- The nominations are closed and all the candidates known.
- Eve of poll.
- Polling day.

Restrictions on election coverage do not end until the close of polls on polling day.

Under the Representation of the People Acts election coverage on radio must be done by giving each political party either 'balanced time' or 'equal time' depending what sort of coverage it is. Balanced time applies when candidates are talking about issues that concern their constituency or when they are electioneering by saying why people should vote for a particular candidate. In national elections the percentage of time allocated to each party is determined by the Radio Authority for independent radio and the BBC Board of Governors for BBC stations, based on the votes cast in previous elections. For example, the three main political parties will be allocated a specific percentage of time, while other candidates, like independents, are given a percentage to share. With the 'also rans' often running into double figures, this usually amounts to no more than a mention of the candidate's name and party at the end of reports or referring listeners to the station's web site for a full list of the candidates.

Balanced time does not mean that every report or discussion has to include every candidate: it means that by polling day stations must be able to show that they have given each party its correct *overall* percentage of time and prominence. An item featuring one party during peak-listening time has to be balanced by other parties being featured at the same time of day. Stations keep track of their coverage in election logs.

Equal time – which means just that – applies whenever party policy is discussed. As Linda Gage points out, 'it is usually easier to organise equal time contributions as a series of programmes' (1999: 144) because within a programme candidates will all try to pick up on each other's statements and a particularly forceful candidate could end up dominating the piece.

The campaign

Generally BBC local radio and commercial stations have a different approach to election campaigns. BBC stations have a higher speech ratio than commercial stations and during election campaigns they are better suited to looking at the issues in depth. As Pete Wilby and Andy Conroy point out,

> Much of the rationale of programming and programme content of many stations during this period is based on notions of listeners' democratic interests, the accountability of political parties and the promises and perspectives of would-be councillors, MPs and MEPs. The station becomes not only the disseminator of news but also the forum for discussion.
>
> (1994: 219)

But while most commercial stations do not cover election campaigns in as much depth as the BBC, they nonetheless endeavour to contribute to the democratic process by providing some information about them. For

example, during the local government elections in May 2000 the Nottingham station, Trent FM, had a campaign to encourage people to make use
of their vote. Managing director, Chris Hughes, says this resulted in an
increase in the turn-out: having a well-informed electorate is important
but of little use unless they actually vote.[8]

In any event care must be taken during the campaign period to ensure
all those seeking election are given fair and balanced coverage. Generally
it is advisable not to run programmes involving candidates until the nomi-
nation period is over. Only then can you know with any certainty exactly
who is standing and therefore who has to be included in programmes.
Once nominations have closed a candidate cannot take part in any item
relating to the election unless all the other candidates are included and
given balanced time, or those who choose not to take part have given their
written consent for the item to run without them, and a balanced report
of their activities is included.

Election phone-ins also provide an opportunity for voters to have direct
contact with candidates but these should be carefully handled. Candidates
are not allowed to take part in phone-ins as callers. Where they appear as
a guest to respond to callers, all other candidates must take part or provide
written permission for the phone-in to go ahead without them. Calls to
the phone-in should be confined to comments concerning candidates in
the studio where they are able to make an immediate response.

Phone-ins, like all election coverage, must give balanced time to all the
parties concerned unless they deal with matters of policy when the equal-
time rule applies. As Linda Gage notes, 'The complications of getting the
balance right mean that it is easier and safer to stick to discussions of
policy on phone-ins' (1999: 145).

The campaign period ends the moment the polls open. According to
the Radio Authority,

> Discussions about election issues should finish at the end of the eve of
> poll (the day before polling). A Licence Holder may not publish the
> results of any poll he has commissioned or undertaken on polling day
> itself until the election polling booths have closed.
>
> (News and Current Affairs Code: 15)

This means on the day of polling stations can only refer to weather conditions and whether polling is light or brisk. Restrictions end when the polls
close: 10 p.m. for national elections; 9 p.m. for local elections.

The count

Very few commercial stations cover election counts live, but if it is a particularly important seat they may send a reporter to get actuality and interviews once the result is known. Once the count begins everyone in the counting area must stay there until the result is declared and if recounts are involved this can last many hours.

Stations doing election-results programmes generally start them an hour after the polls close so that the first results occur quite early in the programme. The presenters on election programmes have to have all their wits about them to keep the studio discussion moving, announce results as they come in, and go to live links when they are ready.

It is common practice for the count from several different areas to be held in a central location. Most of these places – e.g. town halls or large sports centres – often have an ISDN line in place and so live links are less complicated than in the days when landlines had to be pre-booked. Reporters covering a count should use the time before the result is announced to get to know all the candidates and their agents and arrange interviews after the result. If the announcement by the returning officer is needed, reporters should make sure their microphone is in position in good time. They also need to keep an eye on how the count is progressing so that they can let the studio know when to expect a result.

The aftermath

The morning after an election is when most stations give prominence to the whole procedure. Many people will not know the final outcome and they want to be brought up to date as soon as possible. Local radio plays an important role at this time because national coverage cannot explain the impact of the results for every area of the country, and local newspapers are still being prepared.

But as Wilby and Conroy point out, 'detailed statistical information . . . makes poor listening' (1994: 221) and can be a turn-off for election-fatigued listeners. For these reasons most stations confine themselves to the highlights reporting the overall result, any major swings or any particularly controversial wins – then they heave a sigh of relief until the next one comes around.

Emergency situations

Radio is at its best reacting to the unexpected. Its ability to change almost instantly its entire output to react to a crisis makes it the medium most people turn to, at least in the first instance, at these times. Whether it is the death of a prominent politician or member of the Royal Family, or emergency situations caused by snow or floods, radio has the ability to react instantly and provide listeners not only with information, but also with comfort by allowing them to share their reactions with each other.

This was most notably demonstrated at the time of the death of Diana, Princess of Wales on 31 August 1997. Her death shocked the country not only because she was the mother of the heir to the British throne, but also because she was a young attractive woman with a reputation for charity work and championing the underdog. Although no longer an official member of the Royal Family since her divorce from Prince Charles, most stations immediately switched their output to the procedure agreed for the event of a death in the Royal Family.

In the week between her death in a car crash in Paris and her funeral service in London, the airwaves were dominated by the story. Music-based stations dropped their normal playlists and switched to low-key ballads. Talk-based stations scrapped their schedules and many ran phone-in programmes that allowed people to express their loss and share their memories of Diana. The issues behind her death – individual privacy, the Royal Family's treatment of Diana, the media manipulation of the tragedy – were also discussed and analysed with experts on the constitution and psychology adding their voices to those of the public.

Although there were accusations both at the time and later that the media in general had hyped up the situation, many people were genuinely distraught at her death and radio in particular helped them to mourn by involving them in the event. Those who wanted to could take part in phone-ins, and others could gain comfort from knowing they were not alone in their grief. Given that details of the accident unfolded over the week, radio was also able to keep people up to date and provide expert analysis of the implications of each new piece of information as it became available.

Although the death of a prominent person is seldom expected, most stations have an agreed format to deal with the situation when it occurs. This includes what kind of music should be played and a list of people to contact who are experts in one way or another and can make useful contributions to programmes. The reason radio deals so well with the unexpected is that it is immediate, and because it is portable it can be accessed anywhere. This was particularly demonstrated during the fuel crisis of September 2000 when protestors blockaded fuel depots and garages across the country ran dry. Many local stations found that the public turned to them for advice on where to get petrol and the police used stations to try to prevent traffic jams caused by drivers queuing for fuel.

Similarly, bad weather conditions can instantly be relayed on the radio and most stations issue special news updates at times of severe snow or floods to let listeners know what routes are closed, what schools are closed, and how to get help where it is needed. Even people who normally do not listen to their local station will tune in at times of emergency to get information that is relevant to their area.

'People tend to think of us as another emergency service,' explains Jane Hill, the programme manager at the Lincs FM group.[9] 'I always think of our public service information flowing through our programming and when it snows or floods or when there's a fuel crisis we'll be there with the information and entertainment as well. It's particularly important in areas like Lincoln where there's nowhere else to get that information. You're not going to get it on television and there's not one newspaper for the whole area so there's BBC Radio Lincolnshire and Lincs FM for really local information. We do it in different ways and I see our services as complementary.'

Working on emergency programming can be exhilarating because the situation is constantly changing and there is a need to get new information out as soon as possible. But no matter how hard-pushed you are, extreme care needs to be taken to make sure the information you are giving is accurate. Wherever possible, information phoned in from listeners needs to be checked with the relevant authorities before it is broadcast. An incorrect piece of information could make the situation worse and if there is any doubt about its veracity it should be left out.

During the September 2000 fuel crisis, for example, Red Dragon FM in Cardiff sparked off another round of panic buying when DJ Warren Moore and newsreader Stuart McTeer told listeners that they had received a number of calls from people claiming another blockade was due to begin that night. The rumour spread across the country and in a matter of hours there were queues at petrol stations. Although a Radio Authority investigation cleared the station of scaremongering, its director of programming and advertising, Martin Campbell, said lessons needed to be learned from the incident. 'These presenters clearly did state that the rumours were unsubstantiated, although I would accept there is an argument to say that they should have stressed that more forcibly,' he said after examining a transcript of the show.[10] 'It also highlighted the dangers of presenters using clichés such as "things can change" as a substitute for absolute knowledge of what is going on.'

The examples above show how keenly radio can influence its audience. Radio is an invisible medium but that does not mean it does not convey images. As mentioned previously, one of radio's most effective means of connecting with the audience is that it gives the illusion of addressing the individual rather than the mass. In practice this means radio tends to regard its audience as a series of individuals that share to a greater or lesser extent similar characteristics. However, as the following chapter discusses, in order to attract a large audience most radio stations in Britain do not attempt to recreate a faithful picture of society in the image they present of themselves and their audience, but instead use stereotypical images, and at times this can lead to certain sections of society being completely left out. The following chapter examines the images of society that radio promulgates.

Notes

1   Quoted in the *Independent on Sunday: The Sunday Review*, 2 September 2001.
2   There are several excellent books about radio drama including *Radio Drama* edited by Peter Lewis; *British Radio Drama*, edited by John Drakakis; and *Radio Acting* by Alan Beck. See bibliography for details.
3   All quotations from Karen Morgan from author interview, December 2000.
4   See comments by BBC editor Kate Squire in Chapter 2.
5   All quotations from Pam Melbourne from author interview, November 2000.
6   All quotations from Dan Thorpe from author interview, November 2000.
7   From the *Sunderland Echo*, 28 November, 2000.
8   From author interview with Chris Hughes, October 2000.
9   All quotations from Jane Hill from author interview, October 2000.
10 Taken from Radio Authority press release available at www.radioauthority.org.uk/Information/Press_Release/00/Red%20Dragon.htm.

8 Radio representations

··

The ubiquity of radio and its widespread use as a secondary medium tend to encourage a less critical approach to its underlying messages than is the case with other media. As Anne Karpf observes, 'Radio is a medium that can be taken neat: as a source of education, information and entertainment rather than as a creator of a distinct ideology' (1980: 42). However, despite its ephemeral nature and lack of visual representations radio contributes to what Denis McQuail calls our definition of social reality: 'the place where the changing culture and values of societies and groups are constructed, stored and most visibly expressed' (1994: 1). This is done both by the voices that are heard in the media (literally in the case of radio) and the way the audience is portrayed.

As discussed in previous chapters, radio stations target specific audiences usually on the basis of social class, age and gender. But as Stephen Barnard observes,

> It is the *interpretation* of this data and the catalogue of assumptions made on the basis of it regarding tastes, interests and propensities that drives the content of programmes and how people are represented (and addressed) within them.
>
> (2000: 222)

This chapter examines the way radio represents age, gender and race – three areas that have traditionally been marginalised by the media in Britain. It ends with an examination of the BBC's World Service, whose programmes give a particular image of Britain to the rest of the world.

Age

As discussed in Chapter 1, the audience most sought after by commercial radio stations falls into the 24–35 age range – the one advertisers most want to reach. In practice output designed with this age group in mind will generally appeal to a much wider audience, but those at either end of it have traditionally been ignored.

In the 1990s, however, there were signs that radio stations were becoming more aware of the needs of a wider audience. While changes made to BBC national stations left many over-50-year-olds without a station that catered for their musical taste, in 1998 a music policy to fill this gap was produced for all local BBC stations. On the commercial side Saga – a company specialising in products for the over-50s – launched PrimeTime radio on Digital One, and at the beginning of 2001 secured the regional analogue licence for the West Midlands. According to Ron Coles, the managing director of Saga Radio, the new Birmingham-based station intends to feature music from the 1940s and 1950s through to the present day – a mix he dubbed 'From Hank to Frank and Bing to Sting' – as well as news and speech items of particular interest to older listeners.[1] Moreover, although Classic FM does not specifically target older people, its easy-listening approach to classical music combined with the person-alities of presenters like Matthew Kelly on the breakfast show and Simon Bates at weekends (with a revived version of *Our Tune*) means many of its listeners are older.

There are several factors influencing this change. The most basic is that the population as a whole is getting older and those over 55 are now recog-nised as still leading an active life, and from a commercial point of view to have disposable income which makes them attractive to advertisers. This demographic shift means the fastest growing age group in Britain is the over-50s and their needs and tastes need to be taken into account for stations to maintain if not increase their audience share.

To a lesser extent changes in the way we use radio, as discussed in Chapter 1, are also influencing programming. Most of us no longer tune into one radio station to the exclusion of all others but channel-hop accord-ing to our needs and moods. The pre-set facility that is now standard on radios makes this easier to do, and the increased range of stations makes it more desirable to 'see what else is on' in much the same way as most of us watch television. This may mean that, while stations will concentrate on their core target audience during the day, evening and weekend schedules will target a wider audience loyal to particular programmes rather than the station as a whole. For example, John Peel's Radio 4 programme *Home Truths* has a much wider audience base than the traditional Radio 4 profile, and the arts and culture programme *Night Waves* on Radio 3 attracts listeners with little or no interest in classical music.

In a similar way more and more stations are trying to attract children to their programmes. Classic FM, for example, has slots during the breakfast and drive-time shows specifically aimed at children. In response to this Radio 3 launched *Making Tracks* in October 2000 with *Blue Peter* presenters Simon Thomas and Matt Baker playing music aimed at children coming home from school. Meanwhile Radio 4 reversed a 1998 decision to axe bespoke children's shows with a new children's programme broadcast in spring 2001, and made broadcasting history by devoting eight hours of its Boxing Day 2000 schedule to the reading of J.K. Rowling's *Harry Potter and the Philosopher's Stone* in its entirety.[2] Not to be outdone Virgin Radio also court a younger audience with a regular phone-in for under-11s in the *Pete and Jeff Show* in the evening on topics ranging from 'what I dreamt about last night' to 'my worst school meal'.

Just as with older listeners there is commercial logic in trying to attract children to radio. Apart from the long-term benefit of enculturating them to radio listening, research shows that parents listening with children, particularly on long car journeys, tend to let the children choose the station 'for peace and quiet' (Hargrave 2000: 14). And even when programming is not directly aimed at children, station managers are aware that many will be listening particularly at breakfast and drive-time and try to ensure the content will be acceptable to a mixed audience.

'All our stations have an extremely high reach with 4–14-year-olds and that's important to us,' explains Jane Hill, the director of programmes for the Lincs FM group.[3] 'What we say is when you're on-air don't just think "would that upset a child" or "would that upset a parent" but "would that upset a parent listening with a child" and the threshold is much higher then. For example with the Austin Powers film *The Spy Who Shagged Me* we called it "Austin Powers 2". I know that children use the word "shag" in the playground, and that parents aren't offended by it – but a parent in the car with a child could be affected by it. It's the embarrassment factor we work on.'

But while some stations are attempting to increase their audience ratings through a more inclusive approach to targeting, the majority still cater for a specific age group. At the beginning of 2001, for example, Virgin Radio announced that it was refocusing its music policy to make it more appealing to what it called the 'musically disenfranchised 30–40-year age group'[4] by playing more music from the 1970s, 80s, and 90s and less chart music. According to the station's programme director, Henry Owens, the changes, based on specially commissioned market research, will make Virgin more distinctive. 'The majority of radio stations have responded to the trend for manufactured music, competing for a younger age profile of 15–24-year-olds and cluttering the market with stations with little point of differentiation,' he says.[5] 'Our listeners do not know what is at number one in the charts, nor do they care.'

Ultimately then, commercial radio strives to identify a gap in the market that can deliver a distinct consumer group. As mentioned in Chapter 1, one of the reasons advertisers were reluctant to spend money in the early days was that before 1990 stations were compelled to serve a wide audience: a well-defined audience is more attractive to advertisers. As an increasing number of stations compete for the same audience, this may mean that on an age basis more segments of the population will be directly catered for, but the same logic works against other traditionally marginalised groups who are still under-represented in mainstream radio.

Ethnic minorities

Traditionally, broadcasts for ethnic minorities in Britain on mainstream radio have been shunted into the less popular times of evenings and weekends based on the perception that those not belonging to a particular ethnic group would switch off if broadcasting for minorities intruded into 'their' time. Indeed, even stations dedicated to broadcasting to an ethnic minority – in the main Asian stations – are relegated to the less powerful AM frequencies. 'It's a poor show that we only have one Asian station on FM in Britain and that's a small station in Bradford,' says Asian broadcaster Don Kotak.[6]

The issues surrounding radio for and by ethnic-minority groups are similar to those facing all broadcasting. In the first place it has to be recognised that there are many ethnic groups in Britain beyond the simplistic 'black' and 'Asian' labels commonly used. Indeed, part of the resentment felt by minority groups towards programmes on mainstream stations is their tendency to 'slide into a homogenising blackness' (Ross 1996: 349) which obliterates differences in culture, religion and language. While this problem can be overcome to some extent by separate programming, there is a danger that all this does is stress the 'otherness' of minorities rather than recognise them as part of an integrated society.

That said, a survey by Skillset, the national training organisation for broadcast, film and interactive media, shows radio broadcasting employs the highest proportion of ethnic minority media workers. Nationally, 7.2 per cent of staff employees in radio and just over 14 per cent of freelances employed in radio belong to an ethnic minority (Skillset 2000: 12), but this statistic can be misleading as it does not reveal how many of those people are actually on-air. The lack of black and Asian voices on mainstream daytime radio may not be immediately apparent to most listeners; nonetheless the fact that there are so few does not reflect well on British radio's representation of its non-white audience.

Many ethnic minorities get around the problem of not having a large enough audience base to succeed commercially by broadcasting as community radio stations, usually on short-term RSLs like Radio Ramzan described in Chapter 2. On top of this there are several stations within the London area aimed at different groups – Sunrise Radio; Choice FM, Brixton; London Greek Radio; London Turkish Radio – and cities with large Asian populations like Leicester, Birmingham and Bradford also have Asian radio stations.

As part of their public service remit most local BBC stations also have some ethnic-minority broadcasting, but in general this tends to be poorly funded and scheduled during off-peak hours. In contrast the BBC's Asian Network is a 24-hour station available in many parts of the country as well as on digital radio, satellite and the Internet.

Based in Leicester and Birmingham with a full-time staff of 27 and a similar number of freelance broadcasters, the station uses the BBC network of local and national stations as well as its own resources to cover the whole country. 'We don't really fit the local radio model anymore – to all intents and purposes we are a network now,' explains the editor, Vijay Sharma.[7] 'Our agenda is that we look at communities of interest wherever they are.'

The programmes cover news, current affairs and phone-ins with an equal split between speech and music. Seventy per cent of the output is in English with the rest in Hindi, Urdu, Gujarati, Mirpuri and Bengali, and evening shows are designed for a younger audience. Despite its success Vijay Sharma admits that trying to cater for all Asians on one station is problematic. 'Looking at the major breakdown in the Asian community as Sikh, Hindu or Muslim is very simplistic because we all have multiple identities – we can be English as well as Asian,' she says. 'In our output we try to pick up as many aspects of the Asian community as we can and try to make sure we are inclusive.'

While separate radio stations at least provide a voice for ethnic-minority groups, the ideal that needs to be achieved is for all radio stations to recognise the diversity of the population they broadcast to and reflect it more fully in all of their programmes.

Gender

The original relationship between women and radio was quite clear – women should listen but not be heard. Indeed, until the 1990s the role of women in radio was largely confined to off-air jobs as researchers and producers or working in factual programmes like news, current affairs and magazine-style programmes. Very few were given high-profile jobs on daytime music programmes or – outside Radio 4 which has a long tradition of women controllers and editors – positions of authority.

The reasons for this are a combination of social and technological factors. As Martin Shingler and Cindy Wieringa (1998) point out, in the early days of radio the public voice – for example in the pulpit or Parliament – was the male voice, and early microphones were designed to deal with the male vocal range and give it more definition. This left an enduring legacy.

> Despite technological developments which drastically improved the sensitivity of microphones and receivers ('speakers'), female voices continued to be excluded from many key areas of radio broadcasting on the grounds that the qualities of the female voice were unsuitable for certain types of programming. This attitude has made a lasting impression on the media industry and it would be naïve to think that 'equal opportunities' has eradicated all trace of this.
>
> (Shingler and Wieringa 1998: 46)

With men doing all the talking, it was only 'natural' that women should be the listeners, and early programmes like the BBC Light Programme's *Housewives' Choice* set the stereotype of daytime listeners as housewives who relied upon radio for companionship and relief from their domestic chores. Depressingly this image persisted for many years as the 1973 franchise application from Capital Radio to the IBA demonstrates:

> In constructing programmes to appeal to women (and to a large extent women as housewives) two things have to be borne in mind . . . Women are sentimental . . . Women are fanatical . . . They are escapist, or they are not sufficiently cold-blooded to enjoy drama which, if taken seriously, would represent alarm and despondency. This is what gives them their bias towards stories about hospitals and against stories about guns; towards local issues (where they can plainly see what is at stake) and away from foreign news (of dubious implication); towards happy endings, but happy endings to sagas which are as grittily tough as they know real life usually is.
>
> (Quoted in Karpf 1980: 47)

One of the few mainstream programmes directed at women throughout this time that went against the stereotype of an emotionally unstable, parochial being of limited intelligence was BBC Radio 4's *Woman's Hour*. Although it began life in 1946 with an aim to 'recreate home life after the ravages of the war' (Feldman 1999: 2), right from the start it also tackled social issues of interest to women with coverage of the Royal Commission on Equal Pay in 1946, a campaign for better wages for homeworkers in 1947, and even a talk about the menopause that prompted an angry memo from the assistant controller in 1948:

> It is acutely embarrassing to hear about hot flushes, diseases of the ovaries, the possibilities of womb removal and so on being transmitted on 376 kilowatts at two o'clock in the afternoon.
>
> (Quoted in Feldman 1999: 5)

Former deputy editor of the programme, Sally Feldman, admits even during the 1960s and 70s feminist issues were barely acknowledged and even in the 1980s there was no feminist agenda. But the programme was (and is) designed to cover areas of special interest to women and favour women speakers from politicians to fashion experts. As Feldman notes, 'Men would be featured only when they had something particular to say to or about women' (1999: 3). Despite an attempt in 1990 by the then Radio 4 controller, Michael Green, to get rid of the *Woman's Hour* name because he felt it alienated the male audience, the programme continues to be produced and presented by women, reflecting what Feldman describes as 'a female per-spective illuminating a limitless variety of subjects and ideas' (1999: 8).

Meanwhile, throughout the 1980s on both BBC and commercial music radio the image of women barely changed. Male DJs dominated daytime schedules acting as companions for what was perceived to be an audience consisting largely of house-bound, isolated women. In line with the more liberal attitudes of the times, however, there was a shift away from domestic chores towards sex. As Rosalind Coward wrote in 1984:

> Nowhere is sexual desire more obviously scripted and stage managed than in the mishmash of music and chat directed at women during the day on popular radio. Sexual desire, attraction and love dominate not just as themes in the music but also make up a large part of the DJ's chatter.
>
> (1984: 145)

The role of the radio DJ was to flirt with the female audience – a role that effectively debarred women from popular-music radio presentation.

It would be comforting to believe that these attitudes belong to the past. At the beginning of the new millennium there are a number of women in positions of authority: dozens of commercial stations have women as managing directors and the head of BBC radio is Jenny Abramsky. Women are also on-air more than in the past with high-profile presenters like Radio 1's Sara Cox and Jo Whiley and Virgin Radio's Harriet Scott proving that when given the chance, women can do the job just as well as men. Moreover, although women, particularly between the age of 24–35, are still the primary target audience of most commercial radio stations, there has been a move away from regarding them as house-bound and isolated: 'housewife's choice' or its equivalent has now been replaced by the 'work-force request' on many stations keen to boost their audiences by being played in factories, shops and offices.

But research by Caroline Mitchell and Kim Michaels shows that male presenters still dominate British radio.

> If one combines the BBC and commercial sectors to get a picture of mainstream UK radio, 14.6% of presenters are female and *32% of stations have no female presenters at all*. Commercial stations aiming at the over 40s were particularly poor and stations promoting particular genres of music (for instance dance or gold) employed mainly men.
>
> (Mitchell and Michaels 2000: 240, emphasis added)

Their research showed that the majority of women on-air in commercial radio worked as co-presenters. 'More often than not, the female commercial radio DJ is relegated to a weekend slot or to being the side-kick for a male anchor' (Mitchell and Michaels 2000: 238). On BBC radio 26 per cent of the presenters are women, with the highest representation in local radio which is more speech/news-based than other stations. At Radio 1 under a quarter of the presentation staff are women (ibid.: 241).

So, despite the general opinion that there are a lot of women on-air created by the hype surrounding a few high-profile women, the fact that almost a third of commercial radio stations have no women presenters at all suggests that there is still a prejudice against women DJs. One of the reasons most commonly cited by programme controllers in defence of this situation is that not enough women apply to them (Mitchell 2000; Gill 1993). In part this can be attributed to the fact that until recently there were few role models for women to emulate, but it is also because the lack of a formal route into presenting can mask discrimination.

Nonetheless the prospects for women getting on-air have improved, although there is still an element of tokenism on many stations. 'It's easier now than it was when I started,' says Trent FM breakfast presenter Joanna Russell.[8] 'A lot of programme controllers thought one female DJ at each station was more than enough and if you worked on breakfast you should just be the girl who does the weather and laugh. When I got my job in York there was already a woman there and the managing director said "I don't understand why we've got two."'

As Mitchell and Michaels' research (2000) indicates, the area where women are best represented in radio is the newsroom. Jane Hill, the director of programming at the Lincs FM group, began her career in news. 'The reason I – and probably many other women of my age – went into journalism rather than presentation was that journalism offered loads of role models,' she says.[9] And while she feels that her sex has never held her back in any way, she admits that radio stations can appear intimidating. 'I wonder if some young women are still being a bit overwhelmed by radio stations full of blokes talking about jingle packages, idents and technical stuff, and thinking to themselves, "I need to learn all this before I can become a presenter",' she says. 'But if you want to do the job and you're good you'll get there. A bit of self-belief is what you need, not a vast knowledge of jingle packages.'

For many women the chance to build self-belief and get actual experience of broadcasting comes from community-based short-term stations

(RSLs). The first women's radio station in Britain was Fem FM[10] that went on-air on International Women's Day in March 1992 for eight days. Since then there have been six other stations in various parts of the country that have given women access to airtime and valuable training, often enabling them to go on to work on permanent stations (Mitchell 2000).

BBC World Service

The World Service began life in 1932 as the Empire Service and was designed as a service for expatriates serving time in the colonies. The onset of the Second World War, however, changed the station's focus and it began to create different programmes for different countries. It now broadcasts in English and 42 other languages, providing a mix of international news, analysis and information on short-wave, FM, and digital radio and over the Internet.

Although an integral part of the BBC, the World Service is not funded by the licence fee but receives a grant from the Foreign and Commonwealth Office. But unlike the US government-funded Voice of America, which is generally regarded as little short of an American propaganda service, the World Service is editorially and managerially independent of the British government and operates under the same Royal Charter as other parts of the BBC, which provides protection from government interference.

Throughout the 1990s the future of the World Service was in constant doubt as changes within the BBC eroded its status. Although its reputation as an accurate, trustworthy broadcaster was not questioned, many regarded it as representing Britain's imperial past and questioned its effectiveness as a global broadcaster in post-Cold War times. The root problem was that the service seemed to lack any clear idea of why it was broadcasting and exactly whom it was broadcasting to. Prior to the political changes of the 1990s the service was regarded as important in that it promoted democracy and human rights in countries where these concepts did not exist, as well as being a source of impartial information in countries where governments entirely controlled the press and broadcasting. But the redrawing of the political map not only made this less necessary, it also saw many previously restrictive countries develop their own private media and erode the World Service audience.

All this forced the BBC to rethink the role of the World Service, and in 1998 it was relaunched as 'the world's reference point' with the focus on providing news to a global audience that built upon its reputation for accuracy and impartiality. Two years later the service had a global audience of 151 million listeners a week. To a large extent this renaissance is due to changes in the way the service can be heard. Although traditionally a short-wave broadcaster, since 1998 it has developed an audience on FM: by 2000 it was available on FM in 110 capital cities around the world and its director, Mark Byford, notes, 'Continued FM expansion is essential if we are to maintain audience levels.'[11]

The service also developed its presence on the Internet broadcasting on-line in 32 languages. 'In partnership with BBC Online, the World Service has created the most accessed audio news site on the web, far outstripping other international broadcasters,' says Mark Byford.[12] 'We aim to make every language service available on the net in audio, and develop world-class multimedia sites in nine major languages over the next four years.'

However, despite increasing numbers of listeners using FM or the Internet to access the World Service, short-wave broadcasting is still very popular, as the BBC discovered when it announced its plan to shut down its short-wave transmitters to the United States, Canada, Australia, New Zealand and the Pacific Islands from 1 July 2001. Listeners across the world formed a 'Coalition to Save the BBC World Service', protesting that Internet listening is an expensive way to listen to the radio and the quality is marred by technical problems, while FM rebroadcasts are patchy and often only have as little as five minutes a day of World Service output. In response Mark Byford claims the short-wave switch-off is a response to the changing way people in developed markets access their media. 'In the US twice as many people listen to us on FM as on short-wave and one and a half million users access on-line each month,' he says.[13] The cuts will save the BBC £500,000 a year in operating costs – money they say will be used to upgrade short-wave facilities in less developed countries.

Although the majority of the World Service audience is in developing countries, it is interesting to note that its news programmes have a 14 per cent audience share in key cosmopolitan groups in Boston, New York City and Washington DC and a million UK listeners, mainly from its overnight transmissions on Radio 4's frequency. This suggests that despite the plethora of radio stations available in both Britain and the United States, there is still a need for high-quality serious news programmes that deal with global issues from a local perspective, because, although most of the service's programmes are broadcast from London, its strength comes from using correspondents who are part of the communities they broadcast about.

Notes

1 Quoted at www.ukradio.com, 26 January 2001.
2 According to a report on the web site for the Radio Academy (www.radioacademy.org.uk) this programme attracted over a million listeners.
3 All comments from Jane Hill from author interview, October 2000.
4 Quoted at www.ukradio.com, 25 January 2001.
5 Ibid.
6 For a profile of the Leicester station managed by Don Kotak see Chapter 1. All quotations from Don Kotak from author interview, October 2000.
7 All quotations from Vijay Sharma from author interview, November 2000.
8 All quotations from Joanna Russell from author interview, October 2000.
9 All quotations from Jane Hill from author interview, January 2001.
10 Ironically British Home Stores radio designed to entertain women shopping in their stores is called FEM FM. As Caroline Mitchell observes, 'Fem has become FEM and "retail radio" is the ultimate in niche radio' (2000: 108).
11 Quoted in the BBC World Service Annual Review, 1999.
12 Ibid.
13 Quoted on the BBC website www.bbc.co.uk/worldservice/schedules/010518_byford.shtml.

9 Accountability

....

All broadcasters in Britain have to work within a framework of legal and regulatory constraints designed to uphold the existing law of the country, ensure levels of taste and decency, and prevent a concentration of ownership that it is believed would lead to a reduction in the range of available viewpoints. The purpose of this chapter is not to provide an exhaustive account of the laws and regulations governing radio, but to summarise the main areas of law that impinge on the day-to-day routines of programme-making, some of which have already been discussed in earlier chapters, and outline the options available for regulating the medium.

Legislative controls

The purpose of legislative controls on radio is to ensure that broadcast material does not work against the interests of justice, unfairly represent a person or organisation, jeopardise national security, or cause offence to individuals or groups in society. In many cases these laws apply to all media, not just radio.

Defamation

The law of defamation is designed to protect the reputation of individuals and groups from unjustified attacks but because there is no absolute definition of defamation this can be a minefield for broadcasters who need to be aware that a careless comment about someone could land them in court.

Broadly speaking, defamation can be caused by written statements or pictures, in which case it is libel, or spoken statements where it is treated as slander. However, under the Broadcasting Act of 1990 any defamatory statement made on radio or television is treated as libel. As Tom Welsh and Walter Greenwood point out:

> Judges tell juries that a statement about a person is defamatory of him if it tends to do any of the following:
>
> (a) exposes him to hatred, ridicule or contempt;
>
> (b) cause him to be shunned or avoided;
>
> (c) lower him in the eyes of right thinking members of society generally; *or*
>
> (d) disparage him in his business, trade, office or profession.
>
> (Welsh and Greenwood 1999: 149)

Reporting restrictions and contempt of court

Restrictions on the reporting of court cases are covered by a series of laws but can also be ordered by judges in specific cases. One of the main reasons for imposing restrictions is to prevent media coverage from adversely affecting the outcome of cases. For example, the 1980 Magistrates' Court Act restricts what can be reported about a preliminary hearing or committal proceedings to prevent prejudicing the full hearing. This limits these reports to specified facts – for example, the names of those involved, a summary of the offence, bail arrangements and the date and place of any adjournment – unless the defendant applies to have the restrictions lifted or the court decides against committing them for trial (Welsh and Greenwood 1999: 33–4).

There are also restrictions to protect the identity of innocent parties involved in reported cases, such as the victims of sexual attack, rape or attempted rape (Sexual Offences [Amendment] Acts 1976 and 1992), and that of juveniles (i.e. those under the age of 18) accused or convicted of offences (Criminal Justice Act 1991). The identification of children involved in family proceedings is covered by the Children Act 1989.

Broadcasters could be regarded as being in contempt of court if their reports were likely to prejudice or give rise to serious impediment of a pending or current court case. This includes making any reference to previous convictions or any extraneous information that could be prejudicial where a case is to be tried by jury. Moreover the Contempt of Court Act 1981 not only covers broadcast reports but also the behaviour of reporters. For example, under section 8 of the Act it is an offence to seek or disclose any information about the deliberations of a jury, and under section 9 it is contempt to use or take into court for use any tape recorder, or to make any recordings, unless the permission of the court has been given.[1]

Official Secrets and DA notices

The disclosure of matters that are regarded as state secrets is covered by the Official Secrets Acts of 1911 and 1989. These are complicated Acts that detail what kind of information should not be reported, as well as restricting the disclosure of information obtained in certain ways, for example if it has been given to the journalist from a Crown servant without lawful authority or in confidence.

Guidance on how certain types of information relating to national security should be reported, or not reported, is given to newsrooms in the form of Defence Advisory (DA) notices. These are issued by the Defence Press and Broadcasting Advisory Committee, which is made up of representatives of relevant government ministries and press and broadcast media. There are six standing DA notices that describe the broad areas that the committee has identified as being likely to require guidance to avoid damaging national security. These cover topics like defence plans and equipment, cyphers and communications systems, and United Kingdom security and intelligence services. Each notice describes what it is seeking to protect and why, but as Welsh and Greenwood point out, 'the system is advisory and voluntary and has no legal authority . . . In effect the system is a code of self-censorship by the press in matters of national security' (1999: 279).

Obscenity

Prosecutions against a station for broadcasting material that may be considered obscene (Broadcasting Act 1990) or likely to incite racial hatred (Public Order Act 1986) can only take place with the consent of the Director of Public Prosecutions. What actually constitutes obscenity, however, tends to change according to the culture and time: the definition of obscene in Victorian times was quite different from that of today. In general, however, material that can be reasonably interpreted as being likely to deprave or corrupt an audience or incite racial hatred is covered by these Acts. Similarly stations can be prosecuted for blasphemy if an item uses language that vilifies the Christian religion or the Bible, or sedition if the item could cause a breach of the peace through the manner in which it is presented.

Regulatory controls

Historically, broadcasting has always been more tightly regulated than other forms of media. In part this is because it is generally regarded as having a more direct impact on audiences than print, but it is also for wholly practical reasons connected to allocating the scarce resource of frequencies.

The Radio Authority

In Britain BBC radio is regulated by the BBC board of governors who control their own transmitters and decide how they should be used. They also deal with complaints about BBC programmes. Under the 1990 Broadcasting Act the Radio Authority allocates licences and oversees national, regional and local independent radio, including non-commercial operations like community radio and RSLs. It publishes codes to advise licence holders of their obligations under the law related to a range of issues and monitors stations to ensure that they adhere to the Promise of Performance stipulated in their licence application. Along with the Broadcasting Standards Commission (see below) it deals with complaints about radio programmes.

The Promise of Performance made by radio stations is what determines their character. This stipulates the ratio of speech to music on a station and outlines what services the station intends to provide, for example through the provision of local news, traffic reports, help-lines, ethnic-minority programmes and entertainment guides. In 1999 the Authority allowed stations more freedom to make changes to their programmes by introducing Formats to judge their performance. This allows stations to make changes to programmes as long as the character of the station remains the same. Under the new system, new stations are required to operate under the more detailed obligations of a Promise of Performance to set the tone and direction of the station before moving to a Format after around six months.

If the Authority finds that a Code requirement, or a Format, or any other licence condition has been breached, it can impose one of a number of

sanctions including fines, the shortening of a licence period, or the revoca-
tion of a licence. In 1999 for example, Huddersfield FM was fined £5,000
for eight separate breaches of their Promise of Performance. In the same
year Xfm in London was fined the maximum amount possible of £50,000
for breaching the Programme Code rules on taste and decency for two
broadcasts which involved the description of a pornographic video containing bestiality. And in September that year Oxygen FM in Oxford had
its licence shortened by two years and was fined £10,000 when it submitted monitoring tapes to the Authority which had been 'mocked up' on air.[2]

The Authority also controls the ownership of commercial radio stations
with rules that prevent certain people or companies from holding or partic-
ipating in licences they grant. These include people or companies outside
the European Union, local authorities, political bodies, the BBC, UK publicly funded bodies and advertising agents. There are also restrictions on
the amount of investment local and national newspapers can have in radio
stations so that a national newspaper group that has a national market share
of 20 per cent or more may not provide a national or local radio service.

Similarly, there are restrictions to prevent an accumulation of interests
in radio that is operated through a complex 'points system'. Essentially
each kind of radio station – national, local and regional – is attributed a
certain number of points and no individual or group can exceed a 15 per
cent share of the radio market.

However, the Communications White Paper of December 2000 could
well change the way radio is regulated. Although at the time of this book
going to press it is still a discussion document, the approach and structures relating to the regulation of radio are close to those suggested by the
Radio Authority in its submission to the Department for Culture, Media
and Sport and the Department of Industry.[3] Under the new proposals the
Radio Authority would be replaced by an overarching regulator for broadcasting and telecommunications called Ofcom within which there would
be 'sufficient flexibility for sector-specific regulation so that, for example,
radio solutions could be applied to radio problems'.[4]

Prior to the publication of the White Paper, the Radio Authority considered five different structures for the regulation of radio. The aim of the
Authority was to find a regulatory structure that would allow the radio
industry to develop and retain its distinctiveness at a time when technological convergence was creating new platforms for the delivery of radio,
and at the same time ensure a plurality of ownership and a diversity of
styles. Technological convergence whereby previously separate services

are bundled together and sold as a package to consumers is now well established. Cable companies, for example, were quick to tempt telephone users away from conventional providers by offering customers a range of services so that along with providing a telephone service they also provide cable television and radio and Internet access.

But while the technology needed to do this is quite straightforward, it has created a blurring of the differences between telecommunications, computing and broadcasting that raises questions about regulation because historically each sector has been structured differently. Regulation of the Internet is virtually non-existent, while that of telecommunication is much lighter than that concerned with broadcasting. So does this mean that if broadcasting moves from analogue delivery to digital delivery its regulation should disappear to bring it more in line with the telecommunications model?

The first option for regulation considered by the Radio Authority was that of mixed regulation. Mixed regulation is effectively the traditional system with a range of independent regulators like Oftel, the Radio Authority and the Independent Television Commission coordinating their work. But while this system can provide a degree of safety from an undue concentration of power in the hands of one body, it is confusing for consumers and operators alike, and might even hold back development.

At the other end of the scale complete deregulation – where economic regulation would be achieved by competition law and content regulation achieved through civil and criminal law – was seen as potentially dangerous. On the commercial side it was believed that deregulation could allow a frenzy of acquisitions and mergers which would undermine plurality and diversity. The Authority also felt that civil and criminal law was not sufficient to protect, for example, minors from inappropriate broadcast material, and that 'matters such as the maintenance of due impartiality and accuracy require a close and immediate regulatory involvement which the courts cannot provide'.[5]

A third structure of bicameral regulation was also considered. Under this structure the regulation of all broadcasting and telecommunications would be separated into two converged regulators to handle content and infrastructure. While this structure might suit companies already established in one or other of these areas, the Authority believed this would cause conflict between the licensing body responsible for infrastructure and the body monitoring content, given that the most effective means of regulating content is the ability to impose sanctions, including ultimately shortening or withdrawing licences.

This led the Authority to conclude that regulation for broadcasting and telecommunications should be carried out by a single body and they considered two structures for such a body. The first was a horizontally integrated body, dubbed 'Fat Ofcom'. Under this structure all licensing, all content and all spectrum management issues would be handled within single departments. But while this structure would allow some flexibility as different media evolve, it was felt that it could work against the interests of radio which could find itself ignored and subject to inappropriate regulation based on the needs of larger media. It was also felt that a 'Fat Ofcom' would represent a huge power base outside government which could run the risk of being accused of being anti-democratic.

Hence the Authority felt the best solution was for a vertically integrated single regulator – 'Thin Ofcom' – which would operate as an overarching, coordinating regulator, overseeing separate sectoral regulators. Under this structure Ofcom would look after general matters while each sector – radio, television, telecommunications and new media – would directly deal with its own regulator. As the Authority explains,

> Sectoral regulators would be able to apply their existing expertise and, in line with the principle of subsidiarity, decisions would be taken as close as possible to the medium in question. This is the most flexible of all the five possible structures for regulation, allowing new media to be accommodated at the appropriate time in their development, contextually sensible regulation to be applied to new media as and when necessary, and for any current responsibilities to be relinquished as required.
>
> (Radio Authority 2000: 32–3)

Although many of the Radio Authority's current duties will be taken over by the new Radio Regulator – for example the licensing of new analogue services, rolling out new digital services and regulating broadcast advertisements – the White Paper also suggests that the regulations governing radio ownership should be relaxed with the current points system scrapped and a 'simpler, fairer regime' introduced.[6]

In a response to the White Paper,[7] the Radio Authority proposes that in any area with a well-developed local radio market there are at least three separate owners of local commercial stations, but where 12 or more ILR licences exist in one area, a company could own up to five licences. In this way the Authority hopes to encourage diversity in radio, not only through a plurality of ownership but also by allowing companies to achieve economies of scale by, for example, having one sales team and management body for several stations with different formats. The Authority also hopes to stop the practice of licences being obtained 'by the back door', by proposing that there should be a two-year moratorium for the selling on of licences together with powers to protect the existing format. Another major change suggested is that local newspapers should be able to own an analogue licence in their circulation area, providing at least one other local commercial service is broadcast in that area.

But while many of the proposals in the White Paper were given a cautious welcome by the Radio Authority – including establishing a permanent community radio sector as discussed below – it had been hoped that they would be more radical, and in particular that the new Regulator would bring the BBC within its remit.[8] In its submission to the government the Authority points out that currently many of the BBC's activities, while not in themselves driven by commercial imperatives, have a direct impact on the commercial radio industry, '[t]hus, commercial radio's main competitor operates without constraints from comparable regulation, distorting the market'.[9]

This is an argument that has long been made by the Commercial Radio Companies Association (CRCA) among others, particularly since changes were made to BBC Radio 2 in the late 1990s when it began to target the key 25–34-year-old audience also targeted by many commercial stations. As Chris Hughes from the GWR group explains, commercial radio operates to a format that is strictly enforced by the Radio Authority, while the BBC has no such constraints. 'I think the way the BBC is just allowed to do whatever it wishes is unfair,' he says.[10] 'They can change their formats, they can launch new services, they can do whatever they wish and the legislation that controls their operations is entirely different from ours. They also claim to be non-commercial animals, which is patently not true at national level, and have a predominance among the transmitter uses in this country which is one of the reasons there isn't as much radio as there should be.'

But despite hard lobbying by the Radio Authority and the CRCA, the White Paper did not suggest any changes to the powers of the BBC board of governors beyond the public having the right to appeal to Ofcom if they felt their complaints about programmes had not been sufficiently dealt with by the BBC. That said, should future regulation develop along the lines suggested by the Radio Authority, a vertically integrated Ofcom would have a flexible enough structure to accommodate the BBC at some point in the future, for example when its charter comes up for renewal in 2006.

Access radio

As mentioned earlier, the development of community radio in Britain lags far behind that in other parts of the world. The promise of the 1990 Broadcasting Act to broaden choice and increase broadcasting opportunities failed to materialise, in part because it did not provide legislative protection for community radio in a commercial radio market. In response to this the Communications White Paper invited suggestions on the development of community media in the UK and the Radio Authority is proposing the creation of a new 'third tier' of radio called Access Radio. As envisaged by the Radio Authority, Access Radio would be fundamentally different from the existing BBC and ILR stations with some broadcasting over a small geographical area on FM and AM, but the bulk of them operating on the Internet or cable.

> The Authority's vision is of a new approach to harness the individuality and potential of non-commercial radio, and of using radio to assist in the broader aspects of education, social inclusion and social experimentation. 'Access Radio' is not designed to be a publicly-funded competitor to small-scale commercial radio, still less to be a way of unsuccessful applicants for small-scale licences finding a 'back door' onto the air . . . The role of the Radio Regulator would largely be to stimulate and facilitate the sector, with a version of traditional licensing applying only in the minority of cases where these stations use broadcast frequencies. The purpose is to enable public access to radio in a new and imaginative way.
>
> (Radio Authority 2000: 17)

The Radio Authority proposes that a special radio fund should be established to help establish access stations with revenue from a variety of sources, including a percentage levy on the national radio advertising revenue of ILR services and a percentage of the BBC licence fee for public service broadcasting.

Reactions to the Radio Authority's proposals were generally favourable and in order to test the viability of the new tier of radio, the authority launched an Access Radio pilot project in January 2002. This involved up to twelve groups being awarded special licences to broadcast for between three and twelve months on both AM and FM. For the pilot project the Radio Authority hoped to attract a diverse range of applicants so that various locations, models and services could be tested to help them to produce guidelines for a permanent community-radio sector. For the pilot the Authority defined Access Radio as follows:

- Projects must demonstrate evidence of social gain and/or public service aims;
- They must be a small-scale neighbourhood scheme or designed to serve a community of interest;
- They must be funded either by a mixture of commercial and non-commercial funding, or through non-commercial funding only;
- They must be not-for-profit or non-profit distributing;
- They must be ring fenced in terms of ownership and operation from Independent Local Radio (ILR) and must be distinct from ILR;
- They must be targeted at and focused on serving the specific neighbourhood or community of interest in question;
- They must provide opportunities to allow the widest possible access among those within the target group to the operation of the service.

(Quoted in Price-Davies and Tacchi 2001: 5)

Information from the pilot project will be used to help formulate legislation and regulations for a permanent third tier of radio of the kind that already exists in many other countries. However, many Community Radio groups feel the Radio Authority's proposals do not go far enough to ensure small-scale, not-for-profit radio can operate within conditions that would ensure its success. In particular the Community Radio Association (now known as the Community Media Association) wanted to make sure that the best model for community radio in Britain was adopted and they commissioned a special report to examine potential models.

The report – *Community Radio in a Global Context* by Eryl Price-Davies and Jo Tacchi – compared the legal and regulatory frameworks for community radio in six countries and put forward a series of recommendations relating to a permanent tier of community licences that take the Radio Authority's proposals a step further.

Its first recommendation is that the term 'Access Radio' should be changed to 'Community Radio' in line with other English-speaking countries and international institutions like UNESCO and AMARC (the World Association of Community Radio Broadcasters). The term 'Access Radio' was primarily adopted because it was felt that existing radio services could argue that they already provide a service to their local communities. But as Price-Davies and Tacchi point out,

> [N]either existing commercial operations or the BBC conform to existing internationally accepted definitions of community radio. Commercial stations are operated for the purpose of making profits, and have a primary responsibility to their shareholders in this respect. The BBC, funded by the licence fee, operates under clear public service guidelines, and these are by no means identical to the ethos of community radio. It is also evident from the research that it would be a mistake to equate 'localness' with 'community'.
>
> (2001: 62)

Based on their research, they define Community Radio as non-profit distributing, designed to serve specific communities of location and/or interest, providing programming that is relevant to the community, and with management structures that are representative of the community the station serves. In order to offer some protection to these stations, they also recommend that commercial groups should be explicitly prohibited from holding the new licences that should be issued for eight years, in line with existing ILR licences. 'This length of time is long enough for a station to develop a reasonable profile in their local area, and to build links with local groups' (2001: 64).

While the report broadly agrees with the Radio Authority's proposals for a radio fund to help finance community stations, it points out that a mixed-funding approach gives stations the strongest financial basis on which to operate, using a central grant from the radio fund as well as money from advertising, sponsorship, grants, hire of facilities and the provision of training activities to other organisations. Commercial operators have argued that allowing community stations to carry advertising could affect their financial stability, but Price-Davies and Tacchi say 'there is no evidence at all in our research that allowing Community Radio to carry local advertising has had any adverse effect on commercial stations operating in the same broadcast area' (2001: 65). They do, however, suggest that in line with the successful community-radio model in Ireland, the overall amount of income generated from a single source should be limited to 50 per cent, and that advertising on community stations should be restricted to events, businesses, services and work available in a specified area only.

The major difference between the Radio Authority's proposals and those in the report stem from how the stations should be broadcast. As mentioned previously, the Radio Authority suggests the majority of these stations should broadcast on either cable, satellite or the Internet. But Price-Davies and Tacchi point out that these delivery systems have low rates of potential listeners and are already available to groups who wish to use them, so FM frequencies should be made available with the possibility of AM only for those who wish to make use of it where no suitable FM frequency exists. Given that many existing commercial operators like Don Kotak of Sabras Sound in Leicester (see Chapter 1) are denied FM frequencies, this could prove to be a controversial point. But as Price-Davies and Tacchi point out, 'All the evidence demonstrates that for this sector [community radio] to be successful it needs to be freely available within the specified broadcast areas . . . thus, FM is the best solution' (2001: 67).

The details of how Community or Access Radio should operate in the UK will no doubt be the subject of much debate before they are finalised. But the encouraging sign is that at least the topic of Community Radio has been brought to the forefront of how radio should be run in Britain, and the advantage of our current lack of community stations is that any model adopted can use the experience of other countries to try to get it right. As discussed in Chapter 2, Community Radio serves a valuable function for both broadcasters and audiences and it deserves to be given the right conditions to succeed.

The Broadcasting Standards Commission

As mentioned earlier, complaints about radio broadcasts are dealt with by the BBC board of governors for BBC programmes and the Radio Authority for independent stations, but there is also a third body that deals with issues of standards and fairness in broadcasting. The Broadcasting Standards Commission is a statutory body that oversees television and radio broadcasts covering terrestrial and satellite broadcasts, text, digital and cable services. Under the Broadcasting Act of 1996 it is responsible for codes of conduct relating to fairness and standards, and it has the power to consider and adjudicate on complaints, monitor research and report on fairness and standards.

The BSC comprises 13 commissioners appointed by the secretary of state for culture, media and sport, who serve on a part-time basis for three to five years. The BSC can only act on complaints subsequent to the broadcast – it cannot preview recorded material and restrict the circumstances in which it might be transmitted. If it considers a complaint to be justified, the BSC may require the broadcaster to publish or even broadcast its findings, but unlike the Radio Authority it cannot fine or sanction a station.

Self-regulation

Although the above section details the formal structures that control radio, there are also less formal ways that stations respond to their audiences. In many ways it is in the best interests of a station to make sure its broadcasts are acceptable to the majority of people and respond to the needs of its audience: a failure to do so could lead to a loss of its audience and potentially jeopardise the future of the station. For that reason and in order to maintain standards most radio stations operate a degree of self-regulation.

As discussed previously, most radio stations operate an ongoing process of internal evaluation with management, producers and presenters meeting on a regular basis to discuss programmes, promotions and audience statistics. This allows any complaints or comments received about programmes to be discussed and evaluated so that a suitable response can be quickly effected. For example, should a particular feature of a programme like a phone-in request slot result in a positive reaction from the audience through comments to the station and an increase in listeners, it might be decided to extend it by either giving more time to it or using it in other programmes. Similarly, should stations receive lots of complaints about the aggressive style of a particular phone-in host and this is combined with a loss of listeners, it might be decided to tone down the style or even replace the presenter.

On top of this, stations respond to audience research about their programmes. As discussed in Chapter 1, this is usually specially commissioned research for independent radio while the BBC receives comments from its radio listeners' councils. Stations also receive feedback from non-statutory bodies like the Viewers' and Listeners' Association.

Hence while legislative and regulatory controls are important, ultimately stations have to keep in touch with their audience in order to be successful. A station that repeatedly faces prosecution or sanctions would soon lose its credibility as a reliable broadcaster and with that its audience, while one that maintains a 'clean sheet' and responds to the needs and views of its audience will thrive. Laws and regulations combined with the practical necessity for stations to win and keep as large an audience as possible – either to attract advertisers or justify the licence fee – all work towards making radio broadcasts responsible and professional.

Notes

1   For more information on contempt of court see Welsh and Greenwood 1999: 124–43.
2   Details of sanctions against radio stations from the Radio Authority Annual Report 1999.
3   For full details of this submission see *Radio Regulation for the 21st Century*, June 2000, available from the Radio Authority.
4   Quoted from Radio Authority press release 'Radio Authority Welcomes Communications White Paper', 12 December 2000.
5   *Radio Regulation for the 21st Century,* June 2000: 30.
6   See paragraph 4.7 of the Communications White Paper, 2000.
7   The response entitled 'A New Future for Communications' published in February 2001 is available from the Radio Authority.
8   The Radio Authority acknowledges that this would require a change in the constitutional arrangements for the BBC as laid out in its Royal Charter, but suggests that mixed regulation could exist until the Charter comes up for renewal in 2006
9   *Radio Regulation for the 21st Century*, June 2000: 29.
10 All quotations from Chris Hughes from author interview, October 2000.

10 Getting started in radio

....

A s the presenter profiles in Chapter 4 show, there are many routes
to getting a job in radio but to work on-air most stations expect
some previous experience and basic technical skills. There are
various ways of getting this experience, as this chapter examines, but all
the radio professionals interviewed for this book agree that enthusiasm,
commitment and a knowledge of the medium are vital prerequisites to
employment.

Finding out about radio can be done by reading books on the subject
and trade magazines like *Broadcast* or *Media Week*, but more important
is actually listening to a range of different stations and programmes to
find out what is available and compare different styles. It is particularly
important to know the programmes, area covered and target audience of
any station you hope to work on, even voluntarily. 'We used to get a lot
of people contacting us to ask if they could help on the programme,' says
Emma Clifford, a producer and presenter at BBC Radio Nottingham.[1]
'They would phone me up and I'd say "What do you think of the
programme?" and nine times out of ten they'd say they'd never listened
to it. That's awful. I want people who've listened not to just one programme but over a period of time so they can come to me and say what
they'd like to do, what their ideas are, what's good and what's bad. You
have to have an enthusiasm for the medium.'

To a large extent the route into radio depends on what area of the
industry you want to work in. Radio engineers and those working in sales
and marketing usually have recognised qualifications, as do those working
in radio journalism. Chris Hughes of the GWR group admits that most of
the journalists they employ tend to come from recognised degrees in broad-

cast journalism (see below). Students from these courses have usually already gained work experience in newsrooms, have a knowledge of the law, technical ability and experience in writing for broadcast and news-reading.

The route for presenters is less clear. Some are recruited from hospital or student radio stations, and others are 'poached' from small stations. 'There are no particular qualifications that are relevant – just a positive indication that you have a "can-do" attitude,' explains Chris Hughes.[2] 'Like other radio groups we spend a huge amount training our people – give us the attitude and we can do the rest.'

Jane Hill, the director of programming at the Lincs FM group, agrees. 'I have yet to discover any course that teaches how to present a live radio programme with personality,' she says.[3] 'Would-be presenters should think carefully before going on a training course when sometimes the best training-ground can be campus radio, hospital radio or RSLs. In hiring presenters we look for people who can talk intelligently about real life and understand the format of the radio station: why we do what we do, and why we don't do what we don't do.'

One of the biggest obstacles would-be presenters face is getting the chance to prove they can do the job. As more and more stations opt for automated output at off-peak times, the chances for presenters to prove themselves on overnight shifts are fewer. But as BBC presenter Alan Clifford explains, getting the experience is a vital first step. 'I don't know how you can convince someone that you would make a good radio presenter without at some point having actually done it somewhere, so you have to do college radio, hospital radio or even pirate radio,' he says.[4]

One way to find out about the industry and judge what area you want to work in is to do voluntary work at a local station. Many local stations have volunteers who help out on programmes, answering phones, greeting guests, helping with production or just making cups of tea. While this is valuable experience and provides an opportunity to see radio from the inside, stations seldom have the staff or time to provide proper training. Once employed most stations provide on-the-job training, but increasingly formal qualifications are provided outside the industry in colleges, univer-sities and through special vocational courses. However, with so many courses available would-be broadcasters need to take care that they select a course that is relevant to the area they want to work in, and wherever possible select one that has a nationally recognised qualification. They also need to consider:

- How the course is assessed. Is it theoretically based or does it give practical training as well?

- What equipment is used? Will it give you skills that are relevant to the broadcasting industry of today?

- Who teaches the course? Do the tutors have radio experience themselves or is it 'second-hand'?

- What links does the course have with industry? Courses that have industry links provide valuable contacts for their students for both work experience and future employment.

- How have previous students fared in the job market? It is a good indication of the relevance of the skills taught on a course if the majority of its students actually get employed in radio on completion.

The following section looks at some of the recognised qualifications available to help people gain the relevant skills and qualifications for working in radio.

National Vocational Qualifications

The first National Vocational Qualifications (NVQs in England) or Scottish Vocational Qualifications (SVQs in Scotland) for media were accredited in 1994. According to Skillset, the National Training Organisation for Broadcast, Film, Video and Interactive Media,

> NVQ/SVQs are qualifications developed by industry practitioners, assessed by qualified industry practitioners and recognised by the industry as a currency to measure competence in the workplace. They have undergone detailed scrutiny to make sure that the qualifications match actual functions performed on the job. It is stressed that the qualifications are based on practical ability in the workplace and not on theoretical knowledge.
>
> (Skillset web page)

N/SVQs can be gained through work experience, production work on a recognised course, or taking part in an industry-led course, but because they are nationally coordinated they all work to the same standard of competence. The coordination of standards for N/SVQs is done by Skillset who are owned by the media industry. It is managed by representatives of the broadcasting and film industries and trade unions and works with key representatives and consultants across the media including the BBC, Channel 4 and ITV.

Skillset deals with training standards for all media, so it is possible to take N/SVQs in a wide range of subjects that allow you to be as general or specific as you choose. Although they do not provide training, they do fund training through their National and Regional Training Consortia and a network of public and private training providers. Their web site at www.skillset.org is a useful starting place for a wealth of information about N/SVQs, where they can be done, and how to apply to do them. It also has information on how to get work experience and has useful contact addresses. Skillset also publishes *A Career Handbook for TV, Radio, Film, Video & Interactive Media* that contains information about what courses are available and what training and qualifications can help with a career in the media.

Radio as an academic subject

There are hundreds of college courses and degrees now available that offer a mix of theory and practice for students keen to enter broadcasting. In most cases radio is studied along with other media. When radio forms a component of media courses up to undergraduate level it usually involves assignments that combine technical competence in production work with the application of communication principles to programme-making. For example, BTEC National Diploma courses in media studies combine different units of skills so that each qualification can be built to the specific interests of each student.

At undergraduate level the number of university courses in journalism, media and communication continues to grow. A Skillset survey in 1996 showed that 120,000 students, counting further education, undergraduate and postgraduate sectors together, were following media studies courses (Lewis 1998: 230). Essentially these degrees can be classed in two ways: those that focus on theory and those that have a strong vocational element.

At the end of the 1990s theoretical degrees like media studies came under attack by sections of the media industry that felt they were of little benefit. The argument was that studying the theory of the media – how they operate, how they are regulated, what effects they have on society and so on – or the theory of communication – how the communications industries are linked, how they are regulated, the history and development of communication and so on – has no relevance to the practice within the industry. Indeed, respected media studies lecturer and a champion of radio as an academic subject, Peter Lewis, admits that he 'used to advise students not to flaunt their media studies too openly among broadcasters, for whom, as I knew, sociology is a dirty word' (1998: 229).

As Lewis has pointed out, the tension between broadcasters and those who plan, teach and study media degrees has arisen mainly because the expectations of those involved are mismatched. Universities, increasingly under pressure to meet intake targets, know that any course with 'media' in its title is likely to be popular. And whatever disclaimers are made by academic planners and lecturers, students tend to believe that taking media studies will help them find a job 'in the media'. Meanwhile the industry is critical of the standards of practical courses and has a deep suspicion of theory courses. What is needed, as Lewis argues, is a more realistic approach to university degrees by both students and the industry.

> Keeping up with the broadcasters is beyond the budget of most univer-sities. Since we cannot promise to match the latest digital system, we should, I believe, be trying to give students the experience of some of the key moments in the creative process – pitching an idea, researching it, planning an item within a programme or recording a short sequence or interview, editing it to a deadline, packaging and presenting it . . . I'd add that in the context I work in – mostly theory – practice along such lines is intended to enhance or explain theory.
>
> (1998: 231–2)

In other words, university degrees in media involve more than a series of training sessions and both students and the industry need to recognise this. As Lewis points out, the simple replication of industry standards by universities has the long-term potential to stifle innovation.

> Nothing is more valuable to both parties in the media studies compact than the broadcaster who has been given the time and theoretical tools to critically reflect on some aspect of his/her work, translating experi-ence into the kind of analysis which asks the awkward questions covered up by the daily rush to meet deadlines, questions vital to the health of broadcasting and society.
>
> (Ibid.: 231)

For those who want to get into broadcast journalism the route is simpler. There are many university courses in broadcast journalism, but the best are accredited by the Broadcast Journalism Training Council (BJTC). This is a body of industry professionals and academic practitioners who monitor courses to make sure they comply with industry standards. This includes making sure the equipment used on courses is up to standard, that the tutors have a background in the industry, and that each course has established links with the industry. The BJTC points out that its recognition 'is valued by teachers and students, employers and employees because its standards are based on direct practical experience, and the training delivered by recognised courses is directly relevant and responsive to the operational demands of the broadcasting industry'.[5]

Most broadcast journalism degrees combine theory and practice and involve students in a work placement at some time during their course of study. The BJTC revisits recognised courses every three years to ensure standards are maintained, and where there is a deficiency it can withdraw its accreditation. A list of undergraduate and postgraduate degrees recognised by the BJTC, and those seeking recognition, is available at their web site at www.bjtc.org.uk.

Other courses

As well as academic courses there are a number of courses in radio skills run by industry bodies and commercial concerns. As with all training initiatives it is advisable for prospective candidates to check them thoroughly before committing to them.

BBC Corporate Recruitment Services,[6] for example, run training schemes in journalism, production and engineering, and the Emap group[7] runs a Modern Apprentice Scheme covering all aspects of radio. It is also possible to get training through bodies like the Community Media Association and the Hospital Radio Association (see Chapter 2). The Radio Authority has a useful fact sheet on careers in radio that is available at their website at www.radioauthority.org.uk.

Networking

No matter what route into radio is chosen, knowledge of the industry and those who work in it is vital. It is useful to get to know people already working in radio to get advice and advance warning of any jobs coming up. As Caroline Mitchell notes,

> Like all areas of the media radio is a highly competitive employment area . . . You need persistence, the ability to gather and use contacts in the industry, to be prepared to do anything (often in a low paid or voluntary capacity) and to seize opportunities as they occur.
>
> (2000: 262)

Technical skills and formal qualifications may provide a good basis for working in radio, but you also need to demonstrate self-confidence and determination. This can often mean being willing to do anything to get initial experience and make contacts, but a flexible approach will broaden your knowledge of radio and can sometimes open up previously unknown areas. It may seem daunting to have to acquire so many skills, but as many in the industry will testify, working in radio can be challenging and fulfilling and that makes any sacrifices and all the effort well worth it.

Notes

1   All quotations from Emma Clifford from author interview, November 2000.
2   All quotations from Chris Hughes from author interview, January 2001.
3   All quotations from Jane Hill from author interview, January 2001.
4   All quotations from Alan Clifford from author interview, November 2000.
5   Quoted on the BJTC website at www.bjtc.org.uk.
6   BBC Corporate Recruitment Services can be contacted at PO Box 7000, London W12 8GJ.
7   Emap 21 can be contacted at Castle Quay, Castlefield, Manchester M15 4PR.

Glossary

....

actuality – the live or recorded sound of an event or interview on location, i.e. as it 'actually' happens

ad – advertisement or commercial

ad lib – unscripted, improvised speech

AM – see *frequency*

analogue recording – recording on to magnetic tape such as reel-to-reel or cassette

as-live – an item pre-recorded to sound as if it is happening live

atmosphere or 'atmos' – background noise that provides a sense of location to interviews or voice pieces. The 'natural' sound of a location e.g. pubs, factories, beaches. Can be used as a 'bed' for studio links to provide continuity to packages. Also known as 'wild track'

audio – literally sound. Material from an interview or a live or recorded voice piece that provides an aural illustration of what is happening

audio feed – sound bites sent to other stations or studios

automatic level control – (ALC) a device on portable tape machines and studio desks that maintains a standard recording level

back-anno, B/A – an announcement given at the end of a piece of music or interview that gives details of what has been heard

band – a separate section on a reel-to-reel tape

base – location of the on-air studio

bed – a recording of music or actuality played under speech to provide continuity or atmosphere. For example the music played under the news on commercial stations is known as the 'news bed'

bi-media – describes any operation that involves radio and television. Both the BBC and ITN have news reporters who serve radio and television

bulk eraser – device that erases the contents of audiotape. Used for 'cleaning' carts or reel-to-reel tape for reuse

bulletin – a report providing the latest information on a topic such as news, weather or travel

cans – headphones

cart/cartridge – a plastic case containing a fixed length loop of tape on a spool. Most commonly used pre-digital recording for news clips, adverts, jingles, etc. Has a function that allows an automatic stop at the end of the recording, then fast-forwards to the beginning again

catchline – word at the top of a script that identifies the story or item; also known as a slug

clip/cut – an extract from an interview or other recording

CMA – Community Media Association

commentary – a report broadcast live from a particular event as it is happening, e.g. sports match, state funeral, etc.

copy – written information read by presenter or news reader. News copy tells the story without any audio

cue – 1. the written introduction to a piece of audio that is either live or recorded; 2. a signal either by hand or by light for the next item to begin; 3. programme or audio played into a person's headphones that introduces or indicates when they should start broadcasting, e.g. from a studio to an outside broadcast unit, or someone on a telephone line

DAB – Digital Audio Broadcasting. Broadcasting using a sound signal made up of discrete electronic units, as opposed to an analogue signal which is a continuous wave form. Provides high quality sound

DAT – Digital Audio Tape. Recording or reproducing using the digital system on a small cassette

delay system – electronic device that delays the transmission of a live signal by three to ten seconds, used mainly in phone-ins to override libels or profanities

demographic – The profile of a station's average listener based on age, gender, profession, race, etc. This is very important to advertisers who want to target a particular audience

desk – the control panel in a studio that mixes different sources for transmission

digital radio – CD sound quality radio that is interference free, delivered over a multiplex that provides a greater choice of stations and can also send data. Requires a digital tuner to be heard

digital recording – sound recorded using a computerised numerical system. Copies can be made of the recording without loss of quality

double-header – item or programme presented by two people

drive – to drive a desk is to operate the studio desk

drive-time – The late-afternoon rush-hour period when a great number of listeners are in their cars going home from work. One of the peak listening times of the radio day

dub – to make a copy of a recording from one source to another, e.g. cassette to disc or disc to cart

duration – length of time to the nearest second of a programme item. The duration of a recorded item should be provided on a label and the cue, along with the 'out words'. The cue should also give the item's total duration, i.e. length of cue plus audio

edit – to make audio ready for transmission. At its simplest this involves finding an appropriate start and end point, but it can also involve removing other unwanted material to help the piece make sense or flow better

embargo – request not to release information until a specified date or time

ENPS – Electronic News Provision Service. The computerised newsroom system used by the BBC to manage audio and text

fader – slide mechanism on a studio desk that opens an audio channel and controls its volume

feature – a prepared item for a radio programme usually consisting of interviews, actuality and links

feed – a supply of audio from an outside source, e.g. IRN feeds news clips to various independent stations every 15 minutes for use in their bulletins

feedback – Also known as 'howl' or 'howlround'. The effect produced when the signal from a microphone is transmitted through a nearby speaker, which is in turn picked up by the microphone producing a high-pitched howling sound. It can also be caused if a phone-in contributor has a radio tuned in to the programme that is near to the telephone

fixed spot – an item that features regularly in a programme at a particular time, e.g. travel news at breakfast and drive-time

FM – see *frequency*

format – the structure and presentation of programmes in an agreed style. The format of a programme will dictate how often time-checks are given or station idents used, and strictly formatted programmes may even dictate the length of links. Formatting provides uniformity of sound across a station's output

frequency – measurement of radio waves. A station's frequency denotes its position on the dial. Frequencies on the AM waveband (amplitude modulation) are expressed as kHz (kilohertz) including medium- and long-wave transmissions, and on the FM waveband (frequency modulation) as MHz (megahertz)

FX – sound-effects used to bring colour to features or packages

GTS – Greenwich Time Signal. Now no longer from Greenwich but generated by the BBC, this is six pips broadcast at the top of the hour to give an accurate time-check

hard disk – computer disk for the permanent storage of material

heads – headlines. The main stories summarised into a few sentences, usually read on the half hour. Also refers to the parts of a tape recorder that erase, record and playback

IBA – Independent Broadcasting Authority. The body that regulated all non-BBC broadcasting prior to the 1990 Broadcasting Act. Replaced by the Radio Authority

idents – a way of identifying the station to listeners. This can either be in the form of a jingle or a simple announcement by the presenter

ips – inches per second. Refers to the speed of tape going past the recording head of a tape machine. Speech is usually recorded at 7.5ips, music at 15ips

IR – Independent Radio – all non-BBC radio covering national, local and regional stations

ISDN – Integrated Services Digital Network. A system of providing high-quality digital audio signals through telephone lines

jack plug – a connecting plug used to route or reroute sources. For example, a 'mini-jack' is used to connect a minidisc recorder to a computer to download audio for editing

jingle – a short musical piece used to identify the station or a particular programme or presenter

landline – a cable capable of carrying a high quality signal used for outside broadcasts before the introduction of ISDN

lead – the first and most important story in a news bulletin; also refers to an electrical cable from one piece of equipment to another

leader – leader tape. This is coloured tape used to show the start and end of a piece of audio on reel-to-reel tape. Traditionally green leader was used at the start, red leader at the end, and any bands in between were joined by yellow tape. This tape cannot be recorded on

LED – Light Emitting Diode. A meter that indicates volume through a series of lights

level – the volume of recorded or broadcast sound as registered on a meter; also a pre-recording check on a speaker's voice, known as a 'level check'

link – any speech between items that introduces or sets up the item for listeners

log – a recording of all the station's output on slow-speed audio or video tape, or on to computer disk. Stations are required to keep this for a minimum period in case of legal disputes; the log also refers to a note of all music played for notification to the Performing Rights Society so that royalties can be paid

Marantz – portable recording machine that uses cassette tapes

meter – device for monitoring audio level. The VU (volume unit) meter gives an average reading of the audio, the PPM (peak programme meter) measures the peaks of the audio

mike rattle – noise caused on tape when the microphone cable is moved during recording

minidisc recorder – digital recording machine that uses a miniature compact disc

mixing – combining two or more audio sources. Used in making packages when interviews and/or links are played over music or special effects

needletime – the amount of time a station may use to play commercially produced music

news agency – an organisation that provides news stories on a commercial basis for use by other news media

news release – also known as a press or media release. Information prepared by an organisation to inform news organisations of their activities. This can be to promote a new venture by the organisation, or provide a statement about an ongoing story like legal or industrial action they are involved in

NVQs – National Vocational Qualifications, known as SVQs in Scotland. A vocational award to a nationally set standard of skill. Standards for radio broadcasting are set by Skillset

OB – Outside Broadcast

off-mike – noise not fed directly through the microphone but audible in the broadcast

out – the last three words of audio on a tape, written on the cue as a warning that the piece is about to end

output – the sound that is heard by listeners

package – a recorded item combining interviews, links, and/or music and effects, prepared for broadcast with a cue

p as b – programme as broadcast. A written record of everything used in a programme, i.e. music, ads, jingles; also known as the log

popping – distortion caused by the rush of air in 'p' and 'b' sounds usually caused by the presenter or interviewee being too close to the microphone

PPL – Phonographic Performance Ltd. Represents record companies and licenses the broadcasting of music

ppm – peak programme meter. Measures the peaks of audio. See *meter*

pre-fade – facility on a studio desk that allows a presenter to listen to an audio source (live or recorded) and adjust the level before it is broadcast

prof – also known as 'in profanity'. When the station's output is in delay, for example during a phone-in, to prevent profanities or libels being broadcast

promo – a promotional spot for a forthcoming programme; also known as a 'trail'

prospects – list of news stories expected to be covered that day

PRS – Performing Rights Society. Represents the interests of musicians, composers and publishers and acts as a clearing-house for the use of their material both live and recorded

psa – public service announcement. Any item that provides information in the public interest, e.g. travel news, notification of charity events, police appeals

Q and A – an item where the presenter asks questions of a specialist correspondent or reporter who has been following a story, and the reporter responds

Radio Authority – the body that licenses and regulates independent radio in Britain

RAJAR – Radio Joint Audience Research. The body owned by the BBC and the Commercial Radio Companies Association that measures audiences for all radio stations in the country

reach – the percentage of total listeners in the TSA (Total Service Area) who tune in during a specified period. See *transmission area*

reel-to-reel – a tape recorder that uses quarter-inch magnetic tape

rot – recorded off transmission. The practice of radio stations recording sections of their own transmission for possible use in later programmes

royalities – fee paid to the Performing Rights Society based on the amount of recorded music played by a station

RSL – Restricted Service Licence

running order – the planned order of items in a programme

schedule – the planned sequence of programmes throughout a week

seg or segue – a sequence of two or more pieces of music broadcast without interruption by a presenter

selector – software system that selects music from a pre-entered base of records. The music is categorised in various ways, for example, artist's name, title, chart position, mood, tempo, etc. and the system provides running orders that take account of the time of day of the programme and the required frequency of play, and makes sure tracks 'flow' together in pace and mood

share – the total listening time achieved by a station expressed as a percentage of the total amount of time spent by people listening to all radio services in the same transmission area

simulcasting – the practice of broadcasting the same output on different frequencies, e.g. analogue stations often simulcast their output on a digital frequency

slug – word or words used to identify an item; also known as a catch-line

sound bite – brief extract from an interview

soc – standard out cue. An agreed form of words used by a reporter at the end of a story, e.g. 'John Smith, for IRN at the Old Bailey'

splicing tape – sticky tape used in editing analogue tape

stab – a short jingle or ident

sting – brief burst of music used to punctuate output

stringer – a freelance reporter covering an area where there is no staff reporter available

talkback – off-air communication system linking studios, control rooms, or OB locations

tbu – telephone balancing unit. Device that provides balance between phone calls being broadcast and the studio output

tease – short advert for something coming up later in the programme or news bulletin

tec. op. – technical operator. Someone who drives the programme from outside the studio

tone – a signal sent before an audio feed to allow levels to be set

top and tail – to make the start and end of a piece of audio 'clean', so that the item starts with the first syllable of the first word, and ends at the correct point

traffic – the department that decides the placement of adverts

trail – a promotional advert for a forthcoming programme

transmission area – the geographical area served by a station. This may not be the same as the area the station can be heard in, but it is the area used by RAJAR to measure a station's audience, and the one referenced to in its output. This is also known as the TSA (Total Service Area) in RAJAR terminology

two-way – another name for a Q and A. An interview between a presenter and a reporter to provide information and analysis of an event

voicebank – system used by the emergency services whereby information is recorded for journalists to access

voice piece – a scripted report of a story read by the reporter, used with a cue read by the newsreader

vox pop – literally 'voice of the people'. A series of responses from people in the street, edited together in a continuous stream. Used with a cue read by the newsreader

VU – Volume Unit meter. This measures the average volume of sound

waveform – the visual display of sound on a computer in digital editing systems

wild track – the recording of background noise or ambient sound on location, used for editing into a recorded piece to provide atmosphere

windshield – a foam 'sock' used over microphones to prevent wind noise on the tape

wire service – national and international news stories sent by news agencies either by teleprinter or computer

wrap – a news item where the reporter links an interview, literally 'wrapping' their voice around a soundbite. In some newsrooms a 'wrap' is interchangeable with a 'package', but it generally tends to be shorter, and often only features one clip

Bibliography

....

Allan, S. (1999) *News Culture*, Buckingham: Open University Press.

Baehr, H. and Gray. A (eds) (1996) *Turning it On: A Reader in Women & Media*, London: Arnold.

Barnard, S. (1989) *On the Radio: Music Radio in Britain*, Milton Keynes: Open University Press.

—— (2000) *Studying Radio*, London: Arnold.

Beck, A. (1997) *Radio Acting*, Oxford: A. & C. Black.

Boyd-Barrett, O. and Newbold, C. (1995) *Approaches to Media*, London: Arnold.

Briggs, S. (1981) *Those Radio Times*, London: Weidenfeld & Nicolson.

Cardiff, D. (1986) 'The Serious and the Popular: Aspects of The Evolution of Style in the Radio Talk 1928–1939', in R. Collins *et al.* (eds), *Media, Culture and Society: A Critical Reader*, London: Sage Publications.

Carter, C., Branston, G. and Allan, S. (eds) (1998) *News, Gender and Power*, London: Routledge.

Collins, R., *et al.* (1986) *Media, Culture and Society: A Critical Reader*, London: Sage Publications.

Coward, R. (1984) *Female Desire: Women's Sexuality Today*, London: Paladin.

Crisell, A. (1986) *Understanding Radio*, London: Methuen.

—— (1994) *Understanding Radio*, 2nd edn, London: Methuen.

—— (1997) *An Introductory History of British Broadcasting*, London: Routledge.

Curran, J. and Gurevitch, M. (2000) *Mass Media and Society*, 3rd edn, London: Arnold.

Curran, J. and Seaton, J. (1991) *Power without Responsibility*, 4th edn, London: Routledge.

Curran, J. and Seaton, J. (1997) *Power without Responsibility: The Press and Broadcasting in Britain*, 5th edn, London: Routledge.

Dougray, G. (1994) *The Executive Tart and Other Myths*, London: Virago.

Drakakis, J. (ed.) (1981) *British Radio Drama*, Cambridge: Cambridge University Press.

Evans, E. (1977) *Radio – A Guide to Broadcasting Techniques*, London: Barrie & Jenkins.

Feldman, S. (1999) 'Twin Peaks: The Staying Power of BBC Radio 4's Woman's Hour', paper delivered at Radiodessy Conference, Cardiff, November 1999.

Fleming, C. (2000) 'Journalism and New Technology', in H. de Burgh (ed.), *Investigative Journalism: Context and Practice*, London: Routledge.

Gage, L. (1999) *A Guide to Commercial Radio Journalism*, 2nd edn revised by L. Douglas and H. Kinsey, Oxford: Focal Press.

Galtung, J. and Ruge, M. (1981) 'Structuring and Selecting News', in S. Cohen and J. Young (eds), *The Manufacture of News*, revised edition, London: Constable.

Gill, R. (1993) 'Justifying Injustice: Broadcasters' Accounts of Inequalities in a Radio Station', in E. Burman and I. Parker (eds), *Discourse Analytic Research: Readings and Repertoires of Texts in Action*, London: Routledge.

Goffman, E. (1981) *Forms of Talk*, Oxford: Basil Blackwell.

Hargrave, A.M. (ed.) (1994) *Radio and Audience Attitudes: Annual Review – 1994 – Public Opinion and Broadcasting Standards Series*, London: John Libbey.

—— (2000) *Listening 2000*, Broadcasting Standards Commission and the Radio Authority.

Hartley, J. (1982) *Understanding News*, London: Methuen.

Hayes, B. (1994) 'The Role of the Public Voice in Present-day Radio', in A.M. Hargrave (ed.), *Radio and Audience Attitudes: Annual Review – 1994 – Public Opinion and Broadcasting Standards Series*, London: John Libbey.

Hutchby, I. (1991) 'The Organisation of Talk on Talk Radio', in P. Scannell (ed.), *Broadcast Talk*, London: Sage.

Karpf, A. (1980) 'Women and Radio', in H. Baehr (ed.), *Women and Media*, Oxford: Pergamon Press.

Lewis, P. (ed.) (1981) *Radio Drama*, London: Longman.

Lewis, P.M. (1998) 'Media Studies: Playground or Passport?', in S. Ralph, J. Langham Brown and T. Lees (eds), *What Price Creativity?*, Luton: John Libbey Media.

McLeish, R. (1988) *The Technique of Radio Production*, 2nd edn, London: Focal Press.

—— (1994) *Radio Production*, 3rd edn, Oxford: Focal Press.

McNair, B. (1994) *News and Journalism in the UK: A Textbook*, London: Routledge.

McQuail, D. (1994) *Mass Communication Theory: An Introduction*, 3rd edn, London: Sage Publications.

Mitchell, C. (ed.) (2000) *Women and Radio: Airing Differences*, London: Routledge.

—— (2000) 'Sound Advice for Women Who Want to Work in Radio', in C. Mitchell (ed.), *Women and Radio: Airing Differences*, London: Routledge.

Mitchell, C. and Michaels, K. (2000) 'The Last Bastion: How Women Become Music Presenters in UK Radio', in C. Mitchell (ed.), *Women and Radio: Airing Differences*, London: Routledge.

Paulu, B. (1981) *Television and Radio in the United Kingdom*, London: Macmillan.

Price-Davies, E. and Tacchi, J. (2001) *Community Radio in a Global Context: A Comparative Analysis*, Sheffield: Community Media Association.

Radio Authority (1994) *News and Current Affairs Code*.

—— (1997) *Ownership Guidelines*.

—— (1998) *Programme Code*.

—— (2000) *Radio Regulation for the 21st Century*, Submission to DCMS/DTI.

Redfern, B. (1978) *Local Radio,* London: Focal Press.

Robertson, E. (1974) *The Local Radio Handbook*, Bath: The Pitman Press.

Ross, K. (1996) 'Multicultural Media: Television for Minorities' Unit 39a, MA in Mass Communications, CMCR, University of Leicester.

Scannell, P. (1991) 'Introduction', in P. Scannell (ed.), *Broadcast Talk*, London: Sage.

—— (1996) *Radio, Television and Modern Life*, Oxford: Blackwell.

Scannell, P. and Cardiff, D. (1991) *A Social History of British Broadcasting,* vol. 1, Oxford: Blackwell.

Schudson, M. (1996) 'The Sociology of News Production Revisited', in J. Curran and M. Gurevitch (eds), *Mass Media and Society*, 2nd edn, London: Arnold.

Seaton, J. (1997) 'Global Futures, The Information Society, and Broadcasting', in J. Curran and J. Seaton (eds), *Power without Responsibility: The Press and Broadcasting in Britain,* 5th edn, London: Routledge.

Shingler, M. and Wieringa, C. (1998) *On Air: Methods and Meanings of Radio*, London: Arnold.

Skillset (2000) *A Snapshot in Time: Employment Census 2000: The Results of the UK Audio Visual Industries First Ever Census*, London: Skillset.

Thompson, J.B. (1995) 'The Theory of the Public Sphere', in O. Boyd-Barrett and C. Newbold (eds), *Approaches to Media*, London: Arnold.

Ward, K. (1989) *Mass Communication and the Modern World*, London: Macmillan.

Welsh, T. and Greenwood, W. (1999) *McNae's Essential Law for Journalists*, 15th edn, London: Butterworths.

Wilby, P. and Conroy, A. (1994) *The Radio Handbook*, 1st edn, London: Routledge.

Winston, B. (1995) 'How Are Media Born and Developed?', in J. Downing, J. Mohammadi and A. Sreberny-Mohammadi (eds), *Questioning the Media: A Critical Introduction*, 2nd edn, London: Sage.

Internet articles

Court, M. (2000) 'Internet Radio Makes Waves', *Electronic Telegraph*, issue 1857, Sunday, 25 June 2000.

Leonard, T. (2000) 'Net Surfers Catch Radio Waves for Record Audience', *Electronic Telegraph*, issue 1813, Friday, 12 May 2000.

Martin-Jenkins, C. (1999) 'Stakes Rise as Talk Radio Makes Waves', *Electronic Telegraph*, issue 1431, Monday, 26 April 1999.

Mills, D. (2000) 'Ad Hoc: Advertisers Going Ga-Ga for Radio', *Electronic Telegraph*, issue 1824, Tuesday, 23 May 2000.

Index

....

References to pages 187-96 are glossary entries; *passim* means scattered references on the pages mentioned. Headings are listed word-by-word.

Guildford College
Learning Resource Centre
Please return on or before the last date shown.
No further issues or renewals if any items are overdue.
"7 Day" loans are **NOT** renewable.

3 1 OCT 2006

2 1 APR 2009

Class: 791·44 FLE

Title: The Radio Handbook

Author: Fleming, Carole.